relationsh*t

Twenty years of awkward situations and questionable choices.

C. N. Mugambi

*relationsh*t*
Twenty years of awkward situations and questionable choices.

This book is based on actual events.
Names have been changed to protect the identity
of individuals depicted in the incidents described.

Copyright © 2011 Christina Nkirote Mugambi
Published in the United States of America

All rights reserved. No part of this publication may be
reproduced, stored in a retrieval system, or transmitted,
in any form or by any means, electronic or mechanical,
without the prior written permission from the publisher.

Author's Note:
Please do not share this information with others who have
not purchased print or electronic editions of this book.
Anyone who think this information is interesting enough
to ask for it, should be encouraged to get their own copy.

ISBN 978-0-9847990-0-8

First Edition: November 2011
Printed in the United States of America

Cover and text designed by Christina Nkirote Mugambi

This book is dedicated

·······

To my father who cheered enthusiastically as I leapt off ledges and to my dear mother who frantically prepared a safe landing.

To my three beautiful sisters; my best friends and confidants.

·······

Forward Fearless Friends!

....

By the time I had written chapter two, I had decided to publish under an assumed name. Because all the events are true, there was not a chance in hell that I would let my work colleagues and childhood friends, or the lady behind the counter at the drugstore handing me a packet of condoms, know that this was my life. No way I was going to risk alienating a future relationship with overwhelming stories from my past. How could I be sure that they would successfully deflect the disapproving looks that accompanied the quiet whispers of their family and friends while valiantly defending my character?

Then I heard it said somewhere that "those who mind don't matter and those who matter don't mind," and realized that I was spending too much time worrying about what people will think of me when they start reading this book. I cannot control people. It doesn't work; I've tried. So all I can do is put forth my best effort and deal with the outcome later.

I hope you find it an interesting read. If you laugh out loud at least one time, or shift uncomfortably in your chair, or cringe, then I did a good job conveying some of the emotions I felt while writing this book. Chances are, if you know me, you'll look at me differently when you make it through to the end ... and that's okay, too.

Contents

·······

1. Nobody expects the Spanish inquisition ... but nobody should subject themselves to it either.
9. So this guy walks into the restaurant with his button-down shirt unbuttoned down to his bellybutton ...
17. I'm not in the business of crushing men's egos, but I have to save face (sometimes).
21. My wardrobe just doubled.
25. Practice makes perfect.
29. I stumbled. And then I fell.
35. Now, I know this heifer did not just dump me on Valentine's Day!
41. Speed Dating 101.
45. There are many reasons I had opted for a penname. Here's one.
53. What Would A Different Deity Do?
59. Driving Miss Daisy.
67. Was that wrong? Really?
71. Let me get this straight ... you want our future kids to worship whom?
79. I should have earned Skymiles for that.
85. Wounded deer.
91. His name was "Cornbread." (Note to self: Never mess around with a grown man who still uses nicknames).
97. Must update my mandate for the next man I date.
103. In my defense: The Grocery Method.
107. The A-1 Steak Sauce Incident.
113. Never ever have I ever.

.... 1 ....

Nobody expects the Spanish inquisition ... but nobody should subject themselves to it either.

The fact that I was responding to a classified ad should have been my first clue, but I guess sometimes I need to be hit over the head to recognize the error of my ways. Can't recall the exact year but I think it was my senior year in college and well into my "I only date girls" season. I will call it a season because it is not a phase; I merge in and out of the straight and narrow path ... a lot. So there I was with my knees tucked under my chin with Southern Voice spread out before me, walking a tightrope between amusement and desperation while reading and scanning and thinking I was really clever in decoding hidden messages that revealed the true intentions of the person on the other end. I didn't know then what I have learned over the years: I always sell myself short and allow people to take advantage of me on my elusive hunt for companionship. Can't blame them when I make it so easy.

My silly curiosity got the better of me because I am always bothered by the thought that I would be forever haunted by not doing something. Anything, really. I was forced to act where not-so-silly people might hesitate. I picked up the phone and called a stranger who had shared nothing about herself apart from wanting to meet a dark-skinned beautiful woman. Did you catch the second flag? I missed it the first time around. The stranger had a type. That doesn't come into play until further into the story when all the pieces fell into place and by that time it was a little too late ... a little like "The Usual Suspects," when the detective is looking around his office and unravels the web he had been woven into.

So … ring, ring. I call this chick and within seconds of composing myself after the awkward hello and explaining that I wasn't a telemarketer but responding to her ad, she starts with the inquisition. "How tall are you? How much do you weigh? Tell me about your complexion. If you were a bar of chocolate, would you be the caramel inside a snickers bar or the color of the chocolate on a mars bar? Do you have any tattoos? How many? Where? Do you have any piercings? Do you have any visible scars or identifying marks? Are you pretty? Who do people say you look like?"

At this point, anybody but me might have already hung up. Not me. Alas, not only did I allow this (what I thought at the time) random questioning to occur, but I answered in full with responses like, "Cadbury's milk chocolate dark," and, "I have dreadlocks and look like Lauren Hill when I do my makeup right." The worst part is that I was giggling like a stupid high school girl while this stranger basically walked me through how to reduce myself into very defined and definite categories. In all this I never asked her anything about herself. For one thing, I really wasn't too interested; I was bored and just wanted a date. For another, I thought that if she noticed that I was not focused on her appearance, her glaring superficial questions would stand out like sore thumbs and she would be embarrassed for ever asking at all. Silly me. The questions then took an interesting turn when she started asking about my living situation and if I am close with my family and how many people I call close friends. I guess my responses were satisfactory because she turned her attention back to me.

When she eventually asked me to describe my eyes and lips I stopped her short. And again, here is a pivotal moment when most would have said goodbye. But here again, I accommodated a stranger at my expense. I told this woman that now she had a pretty good idea of who I was and what I looked like and where I live, and that we should meet in person and allow her to check me out since she was so preoccupied with my physical form. I should point out that at that time I was at my optimum weight so I was also smiling smugly to myself thinking what a prize I would be and how shocked this chick would be that a cute little thing like me had strolled into her life so casually and was about to rock her world.

Date night. I had picked a restaurant in Little Five Points, Atlanta, which was a good 40 minutes from Kennesaw. It was a Moroccan-themed establishment complete with a belly dancer. I wore all black to make my small but very curvy frame look even smaller and spent a good 15 minutes applying my makeup; Miss Hill would have been impressed. Got to the restaurant with five minutes to spare and waited. And waited. I know in the advent of all the wonderful cell phone plans and options available today it seems odd that I didn't call, but back then each and every call cost. And besides, look how cute I look in these boots ... she HAS to show. Which she did, about 20 minutes late. No apology. No excuse. Not even a mention of how hard it was to find street parking (which I still recall it was). She gave me this once over and said how nice it was that I didn't exaggerate too badly and proceeded to order drinks for the both of us.

What's this? She didn't ask what I wanted to drink. Interesting? I've never been here before. Hmmm, shall we stay awhile?

And so I did. I let her order the meal and the evening was going just fine until the bill came and she turned to me and said "You can handle this can't you?"

Well, THIS was new. I didn't know how to process the information, particularly with the waitress leaning over with a raised eyebrow paying close attention to the words that were forming in my mouth. The words that eventually came out were a surprise to her and me both, but didn't seem to faze my date. "Sure, you can get dinner next time." I said with a sweet smile and with cash still in hand, gave my credit card to the eager waitress. As I did some mental math to calculate how many meals this meal had just cost me, a phone call came through on her cell phone that prompted her to leave the table. Let's give her a name, since we've already come this far. So, "Lisa" returns to the table as I am wrapping up with the waitress and says that a friend of hers is up the street and would I like to stop over and say a quick hello before we decide what to do with the night ahead of us. Since I had picked the restaurant, I thought it was a happy coincidence that somebody she knew was in the area and since I am also such a thoughtful and reasonable girl, I offer to drive to the location. Carpooling is responsible, after all.

A couple of lefts here, a right there and several turns later I found myself navigating through an industrial portion of the city. Lisa assured me we were not lost, but made a quick call to confirm the address of the loading dock we had pulled up to. Her explanation about these being lofts that had been converted from an old building made perfect sense. Gentrification was going on all over Atlanta. It didn't seem odd that there were no cars about because it was Saturday night and the residents were probably all out on the town driving European cars and living their wonderful metropolitan loft lifestyles. The big heavy metal door swung open and I walked in and just like that everything changed.

As the heavy metal door shut with a loud thud, I found myself staring at a giant color photo of a woman's vagina. The photo was about my height and maybe 4 feet across. Only once my brain had confirmed what I was looking at did it allow me to observe my surroundings. This was not a loft, at least not a residence. Oh, look! A king-sized bed in the middle of the room with studio lighting around it. More photos of women. That one was tied up with rope but is smiling. A man was walking toward me but had not said a word. Instead his hands were outstretched with his index fingers and thumbs "blocking" me into a rectangular frame with which he viewed me though with his one open squinting eye. He walked behind me and I could hear him muttering "yes" and "great bones" and all the words took on a seedy quality and I felt dirty just hearing them. Then she walked into view. Her name was Rachel. That is her real name; if I knew her last name I would add it here too. Lisa said to her, "this is the one I told you about."

Funny how one moment you can be enjoying a picnic on a sunny day and not notice the rain cloud rolling in. I didn't see it coming but once all the pieces clicked into place it was the perfect storm. I stood there wondering how in the world I would explain this to a judge and if a jury would ever believe my story. After all I was in control right? I answered the ad. I picked the restaurant. I drove to the loft. I walked in ahead of Lisa. So I smiled at the trio while I looked around pretending to take in the art and asked questions about the models while I busied myself in figuring out how would I get out and make it to my car ... and cursed myself for my impractical shoes.

Interesting how in the midst of confusion the mind is able to attain a moment of perfect clarity. Suddenly I knew why Lisa had asked about identifiable marks and if I had close family ties. I understood why she showed up late and had ordered my meal and essentially forced me to pay her bill. And I knew exactly what was in store for me in this place with a man blocking my exit and Rachel telling me why it would be such a shame to scar the pretty face of any girl that didn't follow the rules.

I will say this about my guardian angels – they don't sleep. Partly because I keep them on their toes with all the trouble I find myself in and partly because they know that deep down my intentions are good so they willingly put in extra work to bail me out. My little pals helped me notice something about Rachel: her jacket. I owned the exact same jacket. Had bought mine 2 years earlier and wore it a lot. Enough to notice that Rachel had not gotten around to cutting open the pockets. At first glance the pockets look like a decorative flap, but on closer observation you would notice that the seam could be pulled apart to reveal a deep pocket hidden by the jacket lining. I also knew where she got the garment and how much she paid for it. Being able to notice that obscure piece of information helped me draw some quick conclusions. She was shopping at discount retail stores but she wanted people to think she was important and was trying to project an image that was grander than her situation in life. If she couldn't afford an expensive wardrobe, exactly how many "bitches" did she really have at her beck and call? Sure she was talking about how much money her girls make at private parties and how much she would charge for me because I was in college (and could calculate how much I would be out of pocket on a slow night), but was this really a pimp or an aspirant? That tiny bit of reasonable doubt temporarily numbed my fear and I put my GPA to work.

There was only one plan: get out of the building and into an area where there would be witnesses. I couldn't risk just making a run for it once outside because of my now stupid boots and my car that did not have keyless entry. So I suggested to the group that we should go out for drinks – my treat. Then we could return and take some of the pictures that Rachel wanted to stage on that massive bed. Now, I cannot say with certainty that I gave an Oscar-winning performance, but whatever I said at the time was compelling enough for them to climb into my car and head over to a nearby bar. We got to the bar and the first round was on me. I danced with Lisa and smiled the entire time under Rachel's watchful gaze and bought another round. While they were enjoying their cocktails, I asked Rachel to watch my drink so I could go to the restroom.

Moments after I was heading down I-75 disregarding the speed limit. When the sequence of events played back in my head, and when I recognized what the alternate ending might have been, I pulled off the road to vomit.

As I washed the makeup off my face, I got a call from Rachel. She informed me that her wallet was in the back seat of my car and since it contained over one thousand dollars, I needed to return to the bar. I told her I would courier her property in the morning if indeed there was a purse tucked under the seats.

There was a purse under my seat but no money inside it, just bunches of paper and receipts for childcare. THIS was the pimp that made me hurl perfectly good Moroccan food the previous night? Interesting how much smaller monsters get in the light of day. Interesting that there is no moral to this story, at least not one that I can see. I wish I could say I learned something, but really, how many other times will I ever find myself in the middle of a "trick recruitment drive" for the lesson to be pertinent? All I am able to say is that it happened and it will not happen again.

That is the overarching theme of my experiences; a string of one-off unique encounters that don't offer much in the way of growth, but have significantly impacted the way I walk through this life.

####### 2 #######

So this guy walks into the restaurant with his button-down shirt unbuttoned down to his bellybutton ...

I wish I owned a camera phone back then. I'd have indisputable evidence.

The evening started out like most of my first dates off the Internet with me picking a location that was equidistant for both parties. Because I am considerate like that. The location is also usually inexpensive. Because depending on how things go I might end up going Dutch so I am practical like that. So going into it was pretty much like any other random Tuesday dinner with a stranger. Because that is what people are when you meet them online. Strangers. Doesn't matter how many little flirty winks on whichever dating site you are on, doesn't matter how many instant messages or emails are exchanged. It doesn't even matter how long those phone calls are. Until the first date, those people furiously typing away on the other side of the monitor or breathing heavily on the phone are as familiar to me as the cashier at the grocery store exchanging pleasantries while waiting for me to swipe my debit card. Might see them again. Might never see them again. So I try not to invest myself emotionally too much until after dessert.

That doesn't mean I did not do some due diligence beforehand. His profile revealed that he was an engineer. Check. Was spiritual but not religious. Nice. He lived in Smyrna and approximately fifteen minutes away from me in Marietta. Awesome – won't have to drive too far if things work out. He was not much into sports. Shut up! I get Sundays in the fall? Sign me up. Oh … and he was not interested in having sex before marriage. Perfect.

Sure, I couldn't get a word in edgewise when we talked on the phone. No, I wasn't too concerned that he went on and on about how all the women in his life said he was such a great catch, that anybody who passed him up was insane. Yes, it did strike me as odd that he went to church every single Sunday, so I just assumed he checked the wrong box on religion and left it at that. I wasn't even bothered by his crazy laugh. Because sometimes when I laugh I snort. Everything else after that was just white noise. I was already onboard for our physical meeting.

Leroy was not familiar with the restaurant or even the location. Odd. He indicated that he had lived in Smyrna for five years. The little spot I had picked was dead in the center of a high traffic area. People who didn't even live in the area were familiar with it, because of all their festivals and events held there. I took that in stride, too, and sent the address by text to his phone. In addition to that, I sent him a link to the restaurant's website in case he wanted to check out their menu options.

Homework done. Shower and copious amounts of deodorant plus perfume on (because I sweat a lot). Once my skin had calmed down a bit, I addressed the task of putting on make up to make it look like I didn't have any on. Took forever so I had to call Leroy to beg his forgiveness for running a few minutes behind schedule. He assured me it was no trouble and we pushed back our date by thirty minutes. This was an unexpected treat because now I had extra twenty minutes to play dress up with. It was winter so I was wearing my usual dark grey pants and black form-fitting turtleneck. My long grey wool jacket and pointy black shoes would complete the look. Altogether very smart and flattering. I kept in mind while I dressed that this guy was apparently not having sex so I was not trying to serve my girls up on a platter ... we'd save those for later if things went well.

Five minutes early. Fantastic. Very few cars on the road, so I was not flustered and rushing in late with some lame line about the traffic gods not being kind.

Ten minutes later I had swopped tables and selected one closest to the fireplace. Because I still wanted to look appealing I had opted not to wear any thermal underwear. So taking off my heavy jacket left me a little chilly. I was actually glad he was five minutes late.

Five minutes drag by and I am swirling wine in a glass wondering what the etiquette is for calling a date to find out how much longer they would be. I busy myself with plucking tiny bits of lint off my turtleneck and make a note to self to wash this thing inside out moving forward.

Not sure if I was irritated by what my dryer had done to my almost perfect outfit, or the waitress returning, again, to ask if I was ready to order, but I picked up my phone and called Leroy.

Voicemail? Interesting.

There are certain people who are able to take themselves to the movies alone. Travel internationally alone. Eat at restaurants alone. I am that certain type of person. I wasn't worried that I was potentially being stood up in a public place. I would just have dinner and go home and tell my friends about it the next day. I was worried though that Leroy had fallen victim to some misfortune. So I called again.

Heaven be praised, he picked up! The momentary relief was very quickly replaced with utter confusion when Leroy apologized for missing my call because he was in the shower.

The shower? He was supposed to be sitting across from me fifteen minutes ago. Did I make a mistake? We did push back thirty minutes, but should I have confirmed an actual time?

Leroy did not seem apologetic at all so I was sure that the mistake must have been on my side. He told me he was a few minutes away from the restaurant and would be there in a moment.

I had been sitting in a restaurant for twenty minutes now picking lint off a dining table and trying to smile politely at the hovering waitress. My stomach was empty but my brain was so full. I ordered another glass of wine to drown the questions clamoring for my attention.

How much more of my time was this guy worth? Why am I so intent on meeting him? Was this another "candidate" that I was placing too much stock in because he looked good on paper?

My phone rang and Leroy was on the other end asking for directions.

WHAT?! Did I not text him the address earlier in the day? Did he or did he not just say he was a few moments away?

I pushed all these questions aside and gave him some landmarks to navigate by.

Minutes later - another call.

What does he MEAN he cannot find the building? Why is he rattling on about the shop he is parked in front of? He should not be parked anywhere but in front of the restaurant that is closing in two hours.

I get up from the table and without putting on my heavy coat, I walk outside to see if I can spot his car (he said he would put his hazard lights on). No car in sight. I am surprised that I am actually still on the phone with this guy. Now I HAVE to meet him. I need to find out exactly what an engineer who cannot follow directions or tell time looks like. His photo was a little blurry but he seemed okay. He must be really, really good looking for real. Only ridiculously good-looking men can afford to be this stupid.

Forty five minutes. I don't care who or what the situation is, that has to be an all time record. That didn't matter because nothing else mattered when he walked in.

It wasn't my imagination having a good time with the two glasses of wine in my tummy. It wasn't hypothermia kicking in from standing in the cold directing a disoriented driver. It was the most amazing sight I ever saw. I was stunned but my now screaming mind paused long enough to notice that every other patron was just as captivated. We were all staring at this man who had walked into a fine-dining restaurant with the front of his shirt open all the way down to his abdomen.

And when I say "open" I do not mean merely unbuttoned. His shirt was open in a big "V" exposing his hairy chest and his stomach. The shirt was also striped so the vertical lines were broken by sharp diagonal wings that emphasized the vast expanse of nakedness even more. His shirt collar was flattened onto his shoulders like a miniature cape, causing the "V" to be wider than it ever needed to be and also indicated that Leroy had intentionally and purposely dressed himself that way. The sleeves rolled up to his elbows reinforced this conclusion.

There are certain people who cannot hide their facial expressions. When they are happy, you can see the glint in their eyes, even when they are not smiling. When they are mad, the anger is all over their faces. I used to be one of them. However, in the last few years, I have discovered that I have become very efficient in masking my expressions. Being stunned did not stop the muscles in my face from doing what they had been trained to do on so many first-time dates. I smiled warmly as I gave Leroy a little hug and said cheerfully how nice it was to meet him. I made sure my salutation was loud enough for the closest tables to hear clearly that this was our first encounter. If they were going to retell the story, why leave out the best bit ... this was virgin territory for all of us.

The mind is a crafty thing; it only allows you to navigate one major hurdle at a time. I was so busy reconciling the half-dressed man in front of me that I hadn't looked at his face. Physically there was nothing wrong with his face. It was what he had done to his features that finally silenced my brain. This guy had shaved his facial hair into what I can only call a Tribute to Hitler mustache.

Picture a man with a cleanly shaved face. Now grab a black marker and draw a thin vertical line from the center of one nostril down towards his mouth. Stop. It has to be equidistant between his nose and his top lip. Okay. Now, draw a perfectly horizontal line from that point that extends the length of his mouth. I am well aware that the human mouth curves but those were not the instructions. It has to be an "L." If you envisioned something different, scrap that image and start over. Right. Now repeat on the other side of the face to complete the picture. So precise was the execution that I had to concede that Leroy must be an engineer.

I then sat back and took it all in. He talked about how tucked away the restaurant was making it difficult to find, to which he attributed being tardy. I had to interject and point out that I had been waiting for close to one hour and said jokingly that dinner was on him. He did not respond to that but chatted away about how parking was virtually impossible. He went on to say the most astonishing thing somebody in his position could ever say: "I really don't like being late because I cannot stand people who waste my time. That is just rude and disrespectful." I asked him what else he could not tolerate. He talked. I wasn't listening. I was distracted by the two extra guests he brought to the table, and while his chest was periodically catching me off guard, the tribute on his face was particularly dazzling.

There is no way in hell you are going to kiss a face with that mustache. Ever. All the voices in my head said in perfect unison.

Hovering waitress came back around and proclaimed the kitchen would be closing soon so if we were going to order, this was the time. Leroy picked up the menu looked at it for a couple of seconds and said, "Too steep for my blood, I'll just have water." Cheap bastard. The entrees cost less than fifteen dollars. That was a secondary thought overshadowed by fact that this person got dressed only partially and thought it was sufficient. Even that was trumped by my primary thought: This thirty-seven year old man stood in front of his bathroom mirror holding his razor in one hand while using the other to brush away trimmed hair, and all the while observing his creation ... and saw it was good.

Never going to wake up next to it. Never going to introduce it to friends or family. Never take it to a business-networking event.

Irritated waitress looked at me, probably thinking I was going to ask for water with lemon. I saw the relief on her face when I ordered my meal with no substitutions and an extra side item.

"Would you bring me an empty plate so I can help her with that?"

And just like that I welcomed the waitress into the little club of those individuals who can mask their feelings and conceal their facial expressions. We exchanged a smile and I turned my full attention back to my party. And just as if a whistle had been blown, all the tenants in my head (with their mouths wide open) were jockeying for position. They pushed their way to the front of my consciousness to demand answers.

What the hell? Why are you not calling him on that?
Are you going to sit here and let this stranger waste more of your time?
Can this guy even begin to calculate how much time I spent to look casual, but cute?
Can we please, please have a second date and invite one other person so they can see this?
Oh my gosh, is that sweat glistening on his chest under his hair?
How does he dress for work?
How about another glass of wine?

And then my curiosity (which usually renders all reason or common sense void) kicked in and thought *I wonder what will happen when the bill comes.*

That pretty much settled it. I HAD to stay to the end.

.... 3 ....

I'm not in the business of crushing men's egos, but I have to save face (sometimes).

Road trip!

It was winter and we were in Miami. We were all still freshmen in college which meant we packed the car beyond its legal capacity on the drive down and once we got to the hotel, we didn't park anywhere near the reception. What business was it of theirs if more than seven people wanted to share two rooms?

With the exception of a two couples, everybody in the group was single. It was an extended social circle where most everybody knew each other, or at least had heard of each other. That's how I learned about John. I had not noticed him at all in the sea of faces that came crashing into the tiny hotel room to welcome us to Miami. He was a friend of a friend and that friend spoke very highly about him. Maryanne warned that I would be doing myself a grave injustice not to give him a second look.

A vetted candidate.

Armed with this insider information, I looked at John but did not see him. Instead I saw his potential. Isn't that the cardinal sin that all singles commit? We don't date people, we have affairs with their potential. I saw his height and weight, which complemented mine, and knew physically we'd make a good-looking match. I watched how he interacted with others and the quiet, confident manner he carried himself with, which would balance out my manic tendencies. I saw one of the girls, whom I did not know too well, vie for his attention. That made him even more appealing because now he was a highly sought-after commodity. And yes, I saw that too. I saw him looking at me one too many times.

An aspirant.

There was the small problem of not living in the same city or state, but that was not a deal breaker. I wondered if he was calculating the odds of us being a couple? Probably not. He probably had not made it past the tiny shorts and tight little t-shirts that I suddenly started wearing. The only equation he was probably wrestling with at the time was how to figure out a way into those shorts. He was a slow learner. Our holiday break was wrapping up. Outside of a few conversations weighed down by innuendo partnered by coy suggestive smiles; he had done nothing to forward our joint venture. My attention span had been breached. The t-shirts had gone back to being baggy and the teeny shorts traded in for jeans. The come-hither looks slowly transformed into disinterested glances.

Funny thing about people watching is, while we are watching them, somebody is watching us. Maryanne had noticed the change in my hemline and jumped in to pull me out of my apathy. I told her there was nothing there and I was wasting my time. She responded by reminding me that I had already invested a significant portion of my vacation on John so it was in my best interest to reap some returns.

What a good bad friend. Everybody has a Maryanne in his or her life. You know her as the person who talked you into smoking that first cigarette at thirteen. Or justified why you should drink eight ounces of Vodka-spiked soda before playing the violin in front of the entire student body when you were sixteen. Or at twenty-one, got you so hyped that you woke up the next morning with a tattoo and no money in your pocket. They didn't force you to do anything, but their reasons to do things you knew you shouldn't were always so compelling that it seemed illogical (at that moment in time at least) not to jump onboard.

Peer pressure.

It was Maryanne's contention that having sex with John was the only course of action that would improve the situation. That made perfect sense. I cannot recall what she said, but I am sure it was brimming over with facts and figures and notable quotes about seizing the day and advice on regretting the path not traveled. If John was not going to "be a man" about it and make his move, I was going to preposition him. Hurray!

Hmmmm ...

Daybreak to our last night in Miami lay ahead. The adjoining door to the bedroom where five boys were sleeping stood in front of me. Maryanne's inspiring words helped me turn the knob and peer inside and whisper his name into the darkness. A few noisy moments later, John was at the door and the lamplight from the girl's bedroom shone on his face. He really was attractive and we really would make a good-looking couple. The potential was back.

My resolve was replaced with defiance when I heard a few giggles in the background from the girls who were now (thanks to Maryanne) fully caught up on what my mission was. Before John could inquire why he had been summoned I pushed him back and joined him on his side of door.

The Rubicon.

It was an impossible situation. I was now standing in a room with this boy trying hard to ignore the stifled laughter penetrating the thin hotel walls. The boy pressed up against me was embracing the unforeseen change of events surprisingly fast for somebody that had just been roused out of sleep. He was a loud whisperer. Fearing that his attempts to be quiet would wake the boys; I suggested we move our little party into the walk-in closet.

There is nothing sexy or practical about having, or in our case, trying to have sex in a walk in closet that is less than three feet deep, so why fumble over the details.

The morning after a bad night has such a harsh, hard light to it. Or maybe I was just on edge because I knew what would be served up at breakfast. I needed to get away from the spotlight so I figured out a way to kill the story before it sprouted wings and said something that still makes me cringe. When Maryanne asked how it went, I said with a smirk, "I did not feel him inside me so as far as I am concerned we never had sex." The off-color remark was supposed to deflate the situation but to my horror it had the exact opposite effect. By the time we were checking out of the hotel, everybody was talking about it. And the very worst part was that John caught wind of it.

Ego reigns supreme.

I could have set the record straight but instead I calculated which side of the story I wanted to be on and went into unnecessary details about what should have remained private. In an attempt to deflect attention away from my actions I shifted the burden of that night's failures onto John and left him standing there hurt and confused. Probably wondering what he had ever done to be treated that way. Probably waiting for me to apologize.

I am sorry.

……. 4 …….

My wardrobe just doubled.

There is nothing sexier to me than a man putting his hand on the small of my back and directing me through a crowd. Opening doors and the little half-stand he makes when I rise from, or return to a table are equally pleasing. What is not sexy is a man waiting too long after the bill has been presented and only reaching for his wallet after I have already started diving into my purse for cash. Is the meal on him? Are we splitting the bill? Should I ask now? A girl doesn't like to ask these questions. We are already still debating how much farther the evening will go to be distracted by downside of being "independent" women.

Max saved me from this dilemma by being so offended on our first date that I even looked at my purse, that it was established that for our dates, all I needed was my driver's license. I was instructed not to even glance at the bill when it made its appearance. My job was to show up looking cute, ready to enjoy his wonderful conversation and company. He would usher me through restaurants and social events with his hand at my waist, firmly and deliberately indicating my next step like I was his full-size puppet. It dawned on me that I was basically his arm candy. How glorious!

To ensure that I fulfilled my responsibilities and gave him his money's worth, I started doing extra "girly" things like having regular manicures, wearing skirts (as specifically requested) and even a putting a weave into my hair. I had come a long way from baggy jeans, graphic tees and dreadlocks. I embraced my role very enthusiastically because there was one additional requirement: we did not have to talk on the phone or send any emails unless we were confirming a dinner or date. Max was not a phone person. I could not believe my luck. I had won the lottery. After saying "good night" at the end of the evening, that was it until the next time. I didn't have to call to say I had made it safely home ... like I had never driven a car before that date! I didn't have to call to say how much I enjoyed myself and that I was looking forward to a future date. All I had to do was answer the phone when he called and say "yes" if I was available. With the two exceptions of a little hug to say "hello" and his hand propelling me forward, there was no intimate physical contact. No sex. No kissing. Dating without the work!

The calls were very random and infrequent, but since I was not waiting for them, each one was a nice little surprise that came with a little gift in the form of a pre-paid night out. Everything was going along smoothly until ... a puppy.

Max bought a one-year-old, pure-bred Weimaraner. He was calling to cancel a scheduled date because Lola was not house-trained and he didn't want to leave her alone for hours. He went on about how excited he was to own such a beautiful dog and how he was looking forward to long walks in the park and exercising more. He had already attributed Lola to getting up one hour earlier and accomplishing more in his day. I was actually a little relieved because I own two cats and I had not mentioned it before. I told him about my cats and taught him how to pronounce their French names. We ended the call with me promising to call and check on him and his little girl.

What just happened there?

Max and I would not be going to watch a jazz performance. He would be watching a dog. I had gone from arm candy to pet parent and there is nothing sexy about that. The phone conversations morphed from confirmations about a dinner reservation to which pair of shoes Lola had chewed and what pet boarding facility had webcams. Instead of a night on the town Max was now negotiating a home cooked meal so that we (as in the three of us) could spend quality time at his place. I have nothing against a cozy night in. In fact, I would actually prefer that option once I get comfy with the person I am dating. However, I would never invite a man home so that he can enjoy "quality time" watching my cats sharpen their claws on my fur-covered, ripped-up sofa. I love dogs. I really do. What I don't like about dogs is their breath and their need to let you smell it. Why is dog breath always hot? And the souvenir of that breath is their sticky saliva that they feel must be smeared all over you so you can remember them enough to not want to see their parents again.

He told me on our first date that he could not see blue and certain greens and sometimes making out shades of grey was difficult. I had sneakily worn the same grey pants on a couple of occasions and referred to them as chocolate brown or hunter green, depending on the lighting. I felt bad about that, but now that he had stood me up for a third planned night out, I felt nothing. I chuckled to myself that he probably got screwed at the car dealership with his silver Land Rover and then again when he got a silver Weimaraner. Served him right for being so smug about buying a luxury car and the brand-label dog that was technically my replacement.

.... 5 ....

Practice makes perfect.

Some people practice kissing on their hand. At sixteen I wanted quantitative data on how proficient I was at it. As luck would have it, I hung around a lot of boys. I preferred their company to girls'. Girls only talked about boys and I had no real interest in boys, or giggling with girls about boys, so I gravitated toward a group of boys in my neighborhood. The unfortunate consequence of being the girl always spotted in the company of a big group of boys was the reputation that came with it. People assumed that I was being passed around like a little party favor and that all these boys had their turn with me whenever it suited them. When I caught wind of the rumors I officially started dating Adam, one of the alpha dogs to keep the others in the pack at bay and squash any suggestion that I was easy. A year later to get back at Adam for something he did, or said (I bet it was trivial too) I messed around with one of his closest friends, Calvin. Which ironically turned those rumors into legitimate stories. My research on Harry, a third guy in the same circle didn't help matters either.

Harry was just one of the rank and file members of the neighborhood crew. I knew he liked me and I knew that he would not risk having the alpha dogs find out what the nature of my experiments entailed. It was with this knowledge that I boldly suggested to Harry that I needed his help on some research. He was more than happy to oblige. I hadn't exactly given him the option to say "let me think about it and get back to you," because the proposal was made outside his house, when I had made an unannounced visit. This was pre-cell phones and email accounts or text messages that we have all since become so reliant on. Back then, if you wanted to visit a friend, you got up and left your house and walked quite a distance to their house (or used public transport to get there) and if they were home – great. If not, you would leave a message with whomever you found there, to say that you had come by, and whether or not you would be heading back to your house so that they could hunt you down. The only challenge with this system was the probability of a prolonged game of "tag" that sometimes occurred. Sometimes the message wasn't relayed so it wasn't until you saw your buddy again that you discovered the missed opportunity. It was probably due to this likelihood, coupled with the fact that he wasn't good at hiding the fact that he liked me, that Harry said, "yes."

I am not totally soulless. I picked Harry for this research project because I wanted to get the answers that I thought I needed to know. In return he would get the chance to make out with a person he had feelings for. A win-win situation all around. Since we were not an item, there was no need to build up to the moment. The only question I asked was, "Where do you want to do this," despite knowing the answer. We couldn't very well have a kissing fest in his family's kitchen or dining room. Harry motioned to his bedroom very sheepishly and I bounded in, eager to get started on the work at hand.

"How did that feel?"
"Should I use more tongue?"
"Did you like it when I bit your bottom lip?"
"Am I kissing too fast?"

The answers to all these questions were either a nod for yes or a squint of his eye to suggest that he was still considering his response.

Another few minutes of labor followed by data collection. I noticed after a while that Harry was not giving the research the attention it required. He was more focused on the labor portion of our test and not the results. So I conducted a secondary experiment to see if my test subject had been compromised. I would give him what I considered to be a lousy kiss followed by what I thought was really Oscar worthy and then asked, "Which did you prefer?" Because he wasn't focusing on what I was doing and only paying attention to what he was feeling, I could see that Harry was caught off guard and just made a guess. I gather he must have determined he had a 50% chance of getting the correct answer.

Wrong. He picked the first kiss. And with that, our experiment came to a close. Ironically, after about 15 minutes of swopping spit and varying my technique from Hollywood leading lady to X-rated porn star, I had not uncovered whether or not I was any good. I had, however, discovered something that I find still holds true: If you like somebody, you will put up with their third-rate kissing.

I thanked Harry for his time and stood up off the chair that was next to the edge of the bed where he perched. As I let myself out of his room, I called back to him to remember not to discuss what had occurred, because I would have no option but to deny it and he would then run the risk of upsetting Adam and probably getting beaten up. Harry obliged, because that's what friends are for.

.... 6 ....

I stumbled. And then I fell.

I have to give credit where it is due. Kudos to all those "mistresses" of professional athletes and actors that have been bombarding my favorite info-tainment shows like TMZ for giving me the perfect setting for this chapter: "If you don't pull out now, I'm keeping it." How nastily obscene! How perfect!

Apparently I am not the only chick out here who has been doing her level best not to get pregnant. It is more than a job to stay healthy and make sure there is no trace of anything that might get back to you ... or show up at your front door screaming about you being a home-wrecker (such crap!) instead of directing that anger to the man that started the mess. It becomes a responsibility to mitigate the amount of damage created by a selfish man who can't keep his grubby little greedy hands off single girls. So in addition to being given the stink eye by married women, there is a portion of the single female population that has to contend with the ever looming prospect that every "quick one to tide me over the long holiday weekend with the family" might actually last a lifetime in the form of an undesired pregnancy.

The attacks come from multiple sides and sometimes in unnecessary settings like the drug store. I personally take issue with the clerks at the pharmacy who tighten and purse their lips when I ask for a re-fill of Plan B and then demand to see my identification before handing over the goods. Here I am trying to save a marriage and be the responsible party in this affair, and not involve any extra lives in this situation. The condescending bastards should be giving Plan B as a gift with every condom purchase, or at the very least not make so expensive that it almost becomes a punishment. The last time I checked it is cheaper not to pay child support for a baby that has not yet been born, so why the grief, Pharma?

So here I am at the pharmacy, again, having to deal with the same dirty looks and it occurs to me: why can't I have the baby? I know I want a baby. I know my clock screams bloody murder each time I pop one of these pills. Why am I saving HIM and denying myself the very thing I want?

It's not like all my siblings and close friends and cousins and (some) business colleagues are unaware. They know him and they see us together and we've technically been a couple for fifteen years. I actually sighed as I typed that. Fifteen years. That baby would be about to graduate high school.

In all fairness, I am part of the problem. He wouldn't be in the picture if I didn't leave the door ajar. I just didn't see this coming. It wasn't supposed to happen this way.

I came to the United States in 1995 before turning 21 and very excited to be free to forge my own path without adult supervision. While I had not lived a sheltered life, I still was under the assumption that people operated on the same basic rules that I followed. Simple things like, "If you are married, you shouldn't be chatting up a fresh faced college student who doesn't know very many people." It never occurred to me to ASK if he was married because it honestly never occurred to me that he would be asking me out on a date if he were. There was that ... plus he never wore a wedding ring. Two points for me. Trustworthy and observant.

We never did go out on a date. He would drive all the way to my side of town and I assumed that logistically it made perfect sense. My apartment was close to the collage I attended which meant he would never make me late for class. One demerit for drawing that perfectly rational but naïve conclusion. Then one day, I will never forget it, we are lying in my tiny twin-size bed and his feet were dangling off the side and I suggested that we should go to his place the next time so at least he would not be falling out of the bed. He propped himself up and looked at me with a mixture of puzzlement and amusement and said "I'm married." Just like that. Like it was something I had forgotten to buy at the grocery store. "Honey did you forget to pick up on the fact that I am married when you went to Publix yesterday?"

This is where an intelligent woman would have stood up and kicked him out. Instead I made this little "oh" sound and continued to play with the hair on his chest, like the bomb that had just been dropped on my head really had no effect whatsoever. I rationalized that since I had already slept with a married man, what difference was it going to make if I continued to do so? Besides, he had not exactly lied because I had never asked. That little decision not to make a fuss about it pretty much determined the direction that relationship (and without trying to be dramatic about it, ALL my other relationships) took from then on. Ten demerits for giving him the excuse he needed to rob me of a decade and a half of looking for a future baby daddy.

We never discussed his "other" life and I went out of my way to ensure that I didn't put a crinkle in his day. I became the chick who would rush to the door half naked with a smile on my face asking how much time we had together while I helped him out of his shoes because we only had a few precious moments. I became the chick who listened about the challenges he had at work while he complained breathlessly about the stress in his life after sweating all over my tiny bed. I became the chick who agreed to meet in nasty little hotel rooms and use my credit card to check in. I became the chick who pretended it didn't bother her that I didn't know where he lived or that he denied me his phone number. And when that stupid cell phone did ring, I overcompensated by pretending I had something urgent to take care of just so he could have a hushed conversation with his other life about his last appointment running late. I became the chick that got tested for a full panel of STDs to ensure that I was not the individual that made his "other" sick.

And so it went for over a year. When October rolled around bringing with it my birthday and the promise of doing things differently this year I told The Dirty Old Man that I wanted a fresh start without the trappings of adultery. I was going to move into my new year without my past mistakes holding me down. He said "okay" and pointed out that he wasn't forcing me to do anything that I did not want to do. I was free to try my chances and maybe I would be lucky enough to find a single young straight black man who wasn't going to give me AIDS or have a drug problem or a criminal record. He went on to remind me that he was just satisfying my physical needs so why was it important what his marital status was. He reminded me that I was the one calling the shots and he was just so very grateful to have been selected. He told me over and over again how happy he was that of all the men I could have been with, he was the one who had been graced with the honor to be by my side. Do you see the manipulation? I missed it the first time around. It was very subtle. He preyed on my fear of communicable diseases and very craftily planted the thought that I was the one who had initiated this relationship and was in full control of the outcome. The plain truth was, I was afraid of being alone and he picked up on that scent and released the hounds of hell that I proceeded to do battle with for a decade.

By reducing the relationship we were in the midst of to a switch that could be turned on or off at a moment's notice, he had very effectively paralyzed my common sense. Logic dictates that the more time you invest in a practice (like smoking crack) the harder it is to stop. I was happily fooling myself that at any given point in time, I would utter the words "we are done" and that would be the end of things. I envisioned we'd complement each other on the wonderful times shared and move on into our respective lives. That unfortunately was not the case.

I now watch public service announcements against "meth" with a newfound appreciation. The ads are always the same. Healthy young person experiments with meth, all the while saying, "I will do this only one time" and then the ad fast-forwards to him looking horrible and doing despicable things to get another, stronger high. As much as I would love to say my situation is different, it is actually a lot worse than a drug addiction in very substantial ways.

The lying is the worst. Lying to my parents (they knew of him, but not about him). Making excuses to my friends about why I couldn't show up to specific events with my "boyfriend" and then finding creative ways to avoid ever bringing him up in conversation. At times I would say I was single, trying to stop their questioning altogether; that would backfire when they wanted to introduce me to their other single and available friends. Lying to the front desk personnel at the low budget hotel chain when I would check in multiple times in the same month (how many times exactly can a house be fumigated?). Lying to myself that I wasn't getting emotionally invested and was just having fun and exercising my options to be an independent single female in total control of her sexuality. What a stupid lie.

Apparently I am a really good liar because even as I type this, The Dirty Old Man is still in my life and for some reason it makes perfect sense to me to wait just a little while longer.

Where IS that f*cking OFF switch anyhow?

······· 7 ·······

Now, I know this heifer did not just dump me on Valentine's Day!

She knew. The supervisor seemed to know. Even the guy sitting across from me had an all-knowing smirk when her name came up in conversation. I had a really hard time hiding the fact that I would smile like a ditzy lovesick puppy when she spoke to me directly. I was very lucky that we didn't work in the same department because my productivity would have been really appalling. I was in agony every day trying to figure out if she was being nice to me because she liked me, or if she was just a nice person. I couldn't read her face. Another thing she didn't do was smile. She didn't want people to notice the missing front tooth, which ironically was part of the attraction for me.

I don't like perfect. I like people with scars. I want to hear what life did to them and what caused the physical, or mental, damage. I once started sign language classes because I wanted to date a deaf person. I didn't know one at that time, but that was irrelevant. I wanted to be prepared for the eventuality. I grew out of that pretty quickly because I love music and thought it would be torture not to be able to share that passion for sound. I like singers with raspy voices so I cannot listen to Celine Dion, opera singers, or any other pretty voice. There was a time I would take perfectly clean clothes to the laundry because the son of the owner had a terrible stutter and I loved to hear him say things like, "You want this shirt and skirt starched?" The more I smiled at him the harder those "S" words got. I could have told him that I wasn't mocking him. But if he was comfortable, he spoke perfectly well, so that would have defeated my reasons for bringing five dollar clothing in for seven dollar's worth of service.

Yolanda had two things going for her, the missing front tooth and the sound of her grizzly voice. And when that voice asked me to work later than our already late shift, I did not even bring up the fact that I was using public transportation and the buses would stop running soon. Inside I was doing a happy dance because it was a holiday weekend and the skeleton staff was probably going to ditch their posts early, allowing me some coveted one-on-one time.

Dang it. She caught me staring at her again. What was THAT? Did she just smile, or was it a smirk? Aarrrgghh ... I can't tell. Let's get some coffee; this is going to be a long night.

I tried to look disinterested as I asked Yolanda if she wanted anything from the break room which was on the lower level; I wanted to use the elevator ride to compose myself because I couldn't risk her walking into the ladies'. To my horror she said she'd come along. I was going to be in a metal box, close enough so that she could hear me trying to figure out how to breathe casually. I would also have to stand perfectly still to avoid her smelling me.

Oh God, no. The adrenaline sweat is kicking in early. Please dear Lord, please no!

There really is no use. There is no stopping it. When I get nervous I sweat like a highway construction worker in July. And it is not the glistening that bothers me. It is the smell that is a combination of adrenaline and fear, mixed with some other self-defense mechanism designed to keep others at bay. Horrible stuff. And here it was. I quickly grabbed my coffee mug in one hand and my wallet (not that I needed it) in the other and held both objects close to chest level like they were the cones that airport ground crews use to direct planes to their gate. My arms did not move and I proceeded to stand very still in the elevator, praying that Yolanda's perfume was strong enough for the two of us.

Why is she looking at me like that? What is she doing? Oh. My. Gosh. Today? This is when she is going to make a move? When I have lethal pits?

I was so distraught over the sweat that I didn't take the time to acknowledge what was happening. I was about to be kissed by the girl who was not aware that in an hour's time I would be calling a taxi to drive me to an ATM to pay for my ride home. The girl, who was not aware that I had requested my supervisor to switch me from activations (easy as pie) to collections calls (with a wide array of delinquent people screaming at me for hours) so our schedules would align. She had no idea how much I hated working this shift and that being around her for a few minutes at a time was the only reason I would be eating cereal for dinner at 1 a.m. This girl who now had her hand on my hip and was smiling with a giant gap in her mouth.

Wow, what soft lips she has.

Sometimes after I date men for prolonged periods of time, I get caught off guard by the feel of a woman. I pulled away from the shock - but mostly to breathe. She was saying something about mistletoe and tradition but I couldn't hear.

Breathe in. Now breathe out. Breathe in. Smile back. Don't drop your arms. What is she saying? I can't hear. My blood is so loud!

Yolanda was apparently aware that I was taking the bus so she offered to drive me home. I was thrilled that she knew this little bit about me. A little uncomfortable that my roommates would see her drop me off, but she was worth the onslaught of questions that were bound to follow. Besides, nothing could possibly ever be as uncomfortable as trying to inconspicuously mop up sweat by sandwiching my skirt between my thighs.

Christmas holidays passed and the awkwardness faded as our dates became more frequent. The adrenaline sweats were a thing of the past even as we tumbled in my bed. In her car. In the elevator at work. It was great. I eventually introduced Yolanda to my roommates and she started including me into her social circle.

I have a tiny mental scar – I do not like to be put into a category. Maybe that is a leftover from being in an elementary school where we were divided into houses; all my friends always ended up in the opposing house. It was worse in high school when the house colors were based on birth month and I was grouped with a bunch of people based on when their parents had sex! I get very angry filling out forms with fields like "single" or "black, non-Hispanic" or "less than $25,000 annually". So it should not be a big surprise that I cannot stand being referred to as bisexual when I have already been forced to affirm an alternate lifestyle. It has a very unpleasant undertone of being promiscuous.

If I date a man, I tell him I am straight. I never breathe a word about girls because I see that threesome glaze come over his eyes and it is pretty much over when the "how about HER?" looks make their debut. When I date women, I just pray they never ask me. Problem is they always do, so I either lie and say "men are yucky, gross why would I ever date them?" or I tell a half truth and state that I have been attracted to women since I was 10 years old (and leave off the bit about falling for boys too).

My first Super Bowl party and I was going as Yolanda's girlfriend – not a casual date. This was very exciting for me and my roommates who, for years, had watched me try to get into the inner circle of lesbians. We weren't sure if a roster of all the bisexual girls in the area was circulating, but I had been having the worst luck trying to date girls. I had switched bars, changed my appearance from ultra dyke to lipstick les and eventually something in between. I took to hanging out in feminist bookstores. Nothing worked. Santa really came through for me with Yolanda.

Take it easy; you've answered this question hundreds of times.

The evil bitch tricked me! I was in the middle of giving my "men are yucky" answer to one of the guests and another of the girls asked how I felt about dating Yolanda considering she was bisexual. That bit of news was music to my ears and I responded by saying it would work out fine because I was one too. The room cracked up laughing and a different girl dragged a confused Yolanda out of the kitchen to the yard where they poked fun at her for bringing a stray.

Bitches.

That little incident took its toll. Up until that point, I would get a call from Yolanda at 6 a.m. to help me pull on my sneakers and go for a morning run. She had to start her day at 5 a.m. so she would call and rattle off a list of why I should get up. It was a sweet little ritual I looked forward to. I loved hearing her sleepy voice over the phone on her days off when she would still put in the wake up call. The morning after the Super Bowl party, I woke up to my clock reading 9 a.m. and knew things were about to change. I was not going to stand idly by.

I solicited my roommates to help me shore up my sinking ship with a night Yolanda would not soon forget. Menu: perfect. House: spotless. Roommates: evacuating premises at 8 p.m. It was not a cold night, but the fire was going. A mixed CD of her favorite slow music (playlist complements of one of her friends who felt sorry for me and was willing to lend a hand) was drifting through the room. I wore the dress she loved to see me in and had spent 3 full days drinking water. If there was going to be adrenaline sweat, I was going to ensure it was at least not that pungent.

The conversation did not touch on what had occurred in January and I was eager to put that behind us and focus on our future. Yolanda seemed distracted but blamed it on her new job and the early hours that were wearing her down. I countered by offering a full body massage. She agreed that it would help and I quickly ushered her to my freshly prepared room. A while later I lay next to her rubbing my own neck and jaw line and smiled contentedly to myself and reckoned that the now-exhausted and thoroughly satisfied Yolanda would not be going anywhere soon.

I think I pulled a muscle; I cannot turn my head to the left. What is she saying? Why is she crying? Was it THAT good?

I was sitting up in bed now catching the tail end of a well rehearsed "It is not you, it is me" speech. Yolanda was sniffing and stammering about how she needed to be in a genuine relationship and ours felt like a farce. This conversation should have been had while we were downstairs sipping on soup! Not now. Not after she had been calling out my name and the sheets were still damp. Why couldn't she wait until tomorrow? This was ridiculous. I sat there not saying a word and watching her get dressed. I watched her walk out the room and heard her heels on the stairs and listened to the latch snap as the front door closed.

I cannot believe this heifer just dumped me.

.... 8 ....

Speed Dating 101.

Well ... that was NOTHING like Hollywood!
I did NOT feel like the heroine in a cute romantic comedy.

So I get there 10 minutes before the official whistle -- there was a whistle -- and none of the guys wanted to talk. It was like they were saving their "A" game for when the buzzer sounds!

But I am a trouper so I march onward, into a conversation with this guy who is about to open a gourmet pizza place. To be conversational, I mention that I just polished down 2 slices before I walked out the door, to which he replies -- wait for it -- "So you like the taste of crap, do you?"

WOW. WOW!!

It was so insulting and funny at the same time I just snorted and for the next four minutes listened to how great he was and how well his momma raised him. Please note that we get FIVE minutes total and I didn't get to say another word.

Contender #2
A chef in a restaurant in Buckhead. I learned my lesson well. No mention of Papa John's Poo. THIS gem spent our 5 minutes stealing glances from the chick sitting next to me. So basically he was just wasting time waiting for the REAL conversation to begin. Nice!

Lucky #3
Owns a travel company and organizes safaris for singles and seemed so petrified of me that I kept touching the sides of my head to verify that no horns had sprouted to cause such fear in a stranger's eyes. He was so happy when he finished "doing time" that I could have sworn I heard an audible sigh of relief!

Moving right along. No horns. Check. Do not mention "piss-ah" for dinner. Try to be engaging and not just the jump off for the next chick. OK!

Bachelor #4
Is going to tell his family and friends about this crazy chick that wanted to know how a telephone works. Well, maybe next time don't offer up that you are an engineer for Ericsson and then get snippy with ME because you cannot explain in three minutes how my voice sounds the same on mobile, landline and over the net. Whatever. I can explain every facet of MY job!

Saving the best for last #5
Ahhh … our silver lining. Nice guy. The reason I didn't start trying to slit my wrists with a bendy straw. Sadly however, when he got to the chick-who-collects-glances he was so funny and interesting I felt a little cheated like I was the warm up session for this heifer. Yah, I was close enough to the competition I could smell her breath mints! Pissed me off like that line in the Abba song, "I am so lucky, I am the girl with golden hair." WHAT?!! What does that make me with my little press and curl that none of these guys even appreciated?!

So apparently if you have less than 10 "dates" your next event is free. There were only five guys so technically they owe me one but those are chips I will never cash in.

But never fear. I did say I was a trouper right?!

About to get all gussied up for a party tonight and I also have a hot date tomorrow with this really nice guy I've been chatting with for one week. Wish me luck!

.... 9 ....

There are many reasons I had opted for a pen name. Here's just one.

We both would have been better off if we had called it what it was and left it at that. Technically it wasn't a one-night stand. No sex was had. A lot of cuddling and for a strange reason, very little kissing for two people naked in the same bed exploring each other's anatomy. I was perfectly happy being restricted to foreplay with this stranger. I am sure at the time, she was relieved that I hadn't turn out to be a crazy psycho who had lured her out of a nightclub and driven to the outskirts of a city she was visiting for the first time.

It was "Black Gay Pride" weekend in Atlanta and Alison had made the trip down that September with a few of her friends from Chicago. She had met me walking out of the party and casually suggested I should stay a while. I did. We danced and flirted and I joked that she might want to consider going home with me, rather than sharing a crowded hotel room with her girlfriends. Less than 20 minutes later we were driving beyond the skyline of Atlanta and Alison's apprehension set in. She wanted to know exactly how far was Kennesaw from Atlanta. And why I went to nightclubs alone. And how often, exactly, did I pick up women off the streets to take them home. She did not believe this was a first time for me. I couldn't believe this was my first time either as I reflected on how confidently I talked her friends into letting me drive off into the dark. Especially since I was leaving them with nothing but a vague description of a 20-something-year-old, overly eager girl pouring out of a tiny skirt, whose face was partially concealed behind a mass of dreadlocks.

So. No sex was had. I told Alison I just wanted to lie next to her and nothing more. That was a lie. I figured that as soon as we were both naked she would get with the program and we'd both be in for a wild ride that would bring a smile to our faces any time either of us recalled the day. I would have been better off if we had just left it as what it was – a sweet night in the arms of a stranger. But no, I pushed.

The next morning I asked Alison to join me in the shower. I told her it was not sexual at all. That was a lie. I figured that soap and warm water and me washing her body with a sponge would get me further than the previous night. It almost did until she heard the knock on the bathroom door. There are advantages to living with siblings but that particular morning I cursed the fact that I was not financially stable enough to live alone. With the mood circling the drain, there was nothing much left to do but introduce Alison to my sisters over breakfast and drive her back into town.

What was that? I scored points by NOT having sex with her? Alison was on the phone as I was driving back to the suburbs telling me that her friends were really blown away by the previous night's events. They were apparently swooning that I gave her a bath and didn't pressure her into more than heavy kissing and caressing. Interesting. I pushed on and into a strange undefined long-distance relationship.

We talked on the phone when she returned to Chicago and by the time October rolled around she was on a plane back to Atlanta. I was to pick her up from the subway stop that I suggested. Who knew I would be parked one city block away at the wrong exit? She wasn't impressed that I had not done the proper research to figure out how the metro transit system worked and couldn't understand that I had only been on the train a handful of times despite the number of years I lived in the surrounding area. The drive from downtown Atlanta to Kennesaw was long enough, but the silence in the car made it almost unbearable. Our first quiet fight of more to come.

Alison handed me a neatly wrapped gift and said she thought it might be best if she brought her travel plans forward and flew out the next morning. I did not want to hear it. I had been looking forward to finally consummating this quasi relationship and a little disagreement about the exit and entry point to the subway station was not going to get in the way.

More hugging and kissing. No sex. So frustrating.

The phone conversations were a little strained when she got back to Chicago. Alison explained that her gesture of flying down to spend the weekend with me was a very big deal. I told her it was. That was a lie. I didn't see it as one. I had flown to London (in the middle of winter) for sex, so her jumping onto a flight for a couple of hours didn't make an impression. Apparently it was up to me to show her exactly what grand gestures looked like.

My idea was simple. Impress the pants off her. Literally. I knew she was a big fan of Meshell Ndegeocello. That had come up in conversation when I had mentioned that my sister was friends with one of the people that did the musician's public relations and that he had invited me to go backstage when Meshell was performing in Atlanta. Alison was giddy at the thought that I was going to be in the same room as Meshell. So I set into motion events that still bring a sheepish embarrassed smile to my face.

Martin was a reasonably attractive guy. If I was interested in men at that point in time, I might have taken a second look when he would point out all he had to offer me if I gave him the chance. I might have turned a blind eye and not register how smug and arrogant he was. I might have even overlooked the condescending tone that he saved for the women who had the audacity to deny his advances. I told Martin about Alison and how I was sure she would thank me very generously if I were able to facilitate face time with her musical idol. Martin pointed out that Meshell had a performance in Chicago in November and if I REALLY wanted to impress Alison I should invite her to the concert because he could get her backstage.

Without hesitation I agreed to the plan. It involved me flying to Chicago and staying at Martin's condo, which I was told was conveniently walking distance from the venue. I was so busy congratulating myself for the foolproof plan that I didn't stop to ask Martin if there were any strings attached to his kind offer. I knew Martin liked me, so my enthusiastic thanks for helping was probably enough. Wrong. In return for accommodating my request, Martin wanted sex as compensation.

This is the point where most everybody would have slapped the nastiness out of the mouth of the man that made such a proposal, but, to my dismay, I realized at that moment, I am not most everybody. I paused long enough to consider the grander scheme. In the past I had said yes to sex because I thought it was enough that my partner REALLY wanted me. I had said yes because I was a little tipsy. I had even said yes on one occasion because there was nothing better on TV. So why should I say "no" when there was actually more to be gained by agreeing to the tasteless plan? Martin was holding the key to the door that stood between me and a very happy and very grateful Alison, and while frolicking in bed with her was fantastic, I wanted more. So I pushed back and gave my terms for the agreement. There was not going to be any fondling. No kissing or talking. No oral sex. Just straight intercourse. Nobody was to know about the deal and there would be no repeat performances. Whoever said that "the ends justify the means" obviously had never been party to a contract between depraved individuals.

"Ta-daaaah!"

Who says "ta-daah" when standing naked in front of a woman for the first time, or any time thereafter? I assured Martin that his girth was perfect and that I was very impressed by his size. That was a lie. I was mortified that I had just witnessed a penis pump in action and was trying to reconcile the image of this short chubby man standing in the middle of his living room wearing nothing but dingy white socks, waving an alien contraption in one hand while his other hand gestured at the results. Martin pointed to the sofa and I assumed the pre-determined position. A few carefully placed moans and obligatory gasps later and Martin was finished. I jumped into the shower to prepare for some "thank you sex" of my own that was bound to be served up later that night.

Alison was breathlessly saying hello and was beaming the most radiant smile. I was still tightly embracing her when I was distracted by the sound of a familiar name. Stacy. Why was she saying Stacy's name? I pulled back from the hug to see another beaming face standing next to Alison. A quick introduction later and Stacy was profusely apologizing for how awkward it must be for me. I said it was perfectly fine for Alison to bring her ex-girlfriend to the show. That was a lie. Martin had been very specific that our deal was to get one person backstage. I was NOT going to negotiate for this hanger-on. I couldn't understand why she was even there when Alison had confessed on numerous phone calls how this callous woman had broken her heart and cheated on her. The nerve! There was no way I was going to risk Alison being lured back into Stacy's web so I beckoned Martin who was having an animated conversation with some members of the band. When a few of them turned to smile as he headed my way, I cringed a little bit and said a silent prayer that he had not disclosed what I had done to get to the side door. Things got a little uncomfortable when Martin, instead of saying hello with a friendly hug, grabbed two fistfuls of my behind and tried to lift me off the ground. When he finally let me down and I turned back around to introduce him to Alison and Stacy, they both had a very displeased expression on their faces. Lesbians can be so intolerant. I emphasized to both of them that it was thanks to Martin that we would ALL be getting backstage to meet Meshell and smiled sweetly at Alison as Martin whispered into my hair that Stacy was going to cost extra.

While Alison and Stacy were ushered into the makeshift lounge area behind the stage, I listened as Martin listed all the things he now wanted me to do because the original terms of our deal no longer applied. I countered with my own amendments and proceeded to pretend that I was having a good time. Alison (and Stacy) had a great time. I watched as they shared a sofa with Meshell and turned into twelve-year-old schoolgirls, giggling and animatedly recounting what they were doing when a particular album came out and which songs changed their lives. When Meshell got on stage, I proudly showed Alison (and Stacy) how I had scored front row access. I tried to play it off by shrugging my shoulders and frowning while shaking my head when they gave me strange looks because Martin was busily grinding against my body to the music. I told them to ignore him because he was just drunk. I did my best not to react to his touch and instead focused on all the things I was going to ask Alison to do once this ordeal was over.

After the concert, we went backstage to the lounge but something was missing. Meshell and most members of her band ... and Stacy. I was standing next to Alison enjoying this fortunate turn of events. I figured my work was now done and we were soon departing to her apartment where I could get payment in kind for services rendered. Martin announced that the band had gone ahead to the after party and smiled at me while he asked Alison if she wanted to go. I wanted another shower.

Watered down drinks. Music assaulting ear drums. The smell of cheap cigars, cologne and incense. Sandwiched between a wall and Martin grinding against me while I tried to again reassure Alison that there was nothing weird about what she was observing. An hour had passed. No Meshell or band. No Stacy. Alison had called and Stacy indicated she was having a great time and they would be at the club shortly. Two hours later I was finally saying farewell to Martin and walking to the subway station with Alison. She was no longer smiling. She did not want to talk. A long subway ride later we were quietly walking to her apartment.

This was not going according to plan. I woke up that morning telling a close friend that I had the most perfect weekend in store that was going to sweep Alison off her feet and into bed with me. I was now instead sitting in a tiny apartment in front of a tiny table with a cup of herbal tea staring across at a now angry Alison. She was letting me know how upset she was that Stacy had left with Meshell and the band. I had to keep sipping on the very hot tea because I did not want to say what was on my mind. I did not want to scream "Bitch, do you know what I had to do tonight?" I didn't want to yell, "you had better walk yourself into that tiny room and take off those clothes and show me you are thankful for the sacrifices I made for you!" Instead I nodded and agreed it was very rude for Stacy to walk out like that. Alison did not appreciate me saying that and took to Stacy's defense and angrily lashed out and said I was the rude one because I was gyrating all night with a man.

Maybe it was the watered down drinks. Maybe. But having Alison rush to the aide of Stacy's good name and putting me down was too much. I angrily reminded Alison that Stacy was the one who cheated on her. I went on to say that Stacy wouldn't have done half the things I did that night for her. Big mistake. Alison now wanted to know exactly what "these things" were. Maybe it was the watered down drinks. Maybe. In that moment, a little voice said that I should tell her every detail because when she realized the hell I been through for her, she would automatically reward me all night long. Wrong. Alison did not see things my way. She said I had committed a bigger transgression than Stacy ever did. At least Stacy cheated with a woman. Lesbians can really be uncompromising on that sex-with-a-man topic. I slept on a tiny sofa.

Stacy was brimming over with joy recounting the events of the previous night as we sat in the cozy coffee shop. Alison had told her about Martin and I was surprised to find that she was not as appalled as her ex-girlfriend had been. I was nodding to emphasize the points she was making to Alison and parroting every other word or phrase that defended my actions: "Sacrifice" and "selfless" and "physical act" and "no emotional connection" and found myself really liking Stacy a lot more than I had 16 hours earlier. I affirmed that letting Martin grope me in public was okay as long as we all focused on the bigger goal. I should have kept my mouth shut. Alison was livid that I was suggesting that she was now obliged to have sex with me. I told her I wasn't expecting any sex. That was a lie. My entire being was demanding it. I told her I wanted to have sex whenever she was ready, but we couldn't do anything that particular day because as it turned out, I woke up with a yeast infection. Apparently I was allergic to his brand of condoms.

I was standing at the curb outside Chicago O'Hare watching Alison drive off in Stacy's car wondering how things could have gone so terribly wrong.

.... 10 ....

What Would A Different Deity Do?

Never mind what Jesus would do. I need a malevolent god for this. Two decades have passed and still I want to spit every time I say his name. Spineless coward.

I looked around at the faces of my family and neighbors (who were now standing as close to the police truck as they thought was safe) pleading to one of the armed police officers to take the barrel of the AK-47 off my temple and vaguely acknowledged that I probably could have died that day. The problem was that my defiance and anger had not allowed fear or the full weight of my situation to set in. That made it increasingly difficult for my family to negotiate the bribe that eventually secured my release.

HOW in the world did I get myself into this situation?

I'd like to think that I am not the type of person who goes looking for trouble. But time and time again, even I have to question whether I left a spare key under the doormat for trouble to visit my home whenever and however. And so here it was again, going through the pantry and fridge, looking for something to devour.

We were both eighteen. He was walking me home as we talked excitedly our about future plans, with the final term in high school stretched out before us. I had my arm around his waist because I didn't really care what the neighbors thought. After all, I was going to be leaving for America and that created an air of arrogance and recklessness about me. The police truck pulled up beside us and one of the officers asked where we were going. I motioned to the house behind me and said nowhere. The officer inquired as to why I had spoken without permission. He looked at the boy I was with and repeated his initial question. The boy responded by informing the officer he was walking me home. The officer asked what his last name was and the boy answered. A common enough name that quickly indicated his tribe. I was then asked the same and in response I spat out my father's family name. It was not a common Kenyan name and I smiled smugly at that. This name (most probably the attitude that accompanied it) prompted the man armed with an automatic weapon to jump out of the truck.

If you are East African, or have a member of your family actively serving in the Kenyan Police Force, feel free to skip over this next bit:

During the 80's and 90's in Kenya there was an influx of Somali nationals seeking refuge in Kenya. There were also Kenyan nationals of Somali decent. This created an environment where anybody who looked Somali was constantly harassed by local police officers to produce paperwork to prove their right to be in the country. For the unlucky few caught by crooked cops, despite their legitimate claim to refugee status, they had to pay a bribe to avoid unnecessary detention. The situation was allegedly worse for Somali girls who were targeted and in a few cases had been sexually assaulted. It was easy for the police to pick out Somali women in a crowd because even when they were not wearing their distinctive attire and shoes, their facial features, physical build and hair was very different from the average Kenyan.

And we're back.

What did that have to do with me? The neighborhood I lived in had a huge population of refugees. Years of living side by side allowed a melding of culture. I ate their food and wore their fabrics in place of commercially purchased skirts. At the time the policemen stopped the boy, and me, I weighed about 110 pounds and was wearing Somali fabric around my waist and a fresh perm in my hair, all the while giving this policeman a name that was not distinctly Kenyan. Most people think it has Ethiopian origins when they hear it. In retrospect I do not blame them for thinking I was 100 percent Somali. I should have used my surname, but my arrogance wanted to make me anything but common. I sneered at the police officer when he asked where I was from as he was exiting the vehicle. I told him I was Kenyan and my tribe was of no consequence. The boy responded on my behalf volunteering where my family originated as the other two officers exited the vehicle. One of the other officers asked me to speak in my dialect. The other demanded my identification card. I did not appreciate the interrogation and announced that I would be getting into the house because they were wasting my time instead of doing their job. That was pretty much when all hell broke loose.

Kenyan police officers do not take kindly to anybody talking back to them, particularly if that body is not attached to a set of testicles.

The officer who had asked for proof by way of mother tongue was screaming in my face about how they were going to take me down to the police station so my mouth could learn how to talk to men properly. I took the thinly veiled threat for what it was and declared that they were going to have to enjoy the rape of a dead body because they would have to kill me before touching me. That was apparently a cue because they went into action like they were reading from a well-rehearsed script. One officer opened the door to the back of the truck, a second had lifted me off the ground and the third was trying to shove my limbs into the car.

Impressive and scary. Let's pretend this was the first time they had ever done this.

I parted my legs in the air and propped each foot at the corners of the door. Officer number one took the butt of his machine gun and proceeded to ram the side of my knee in an attempt to buckle my legs. I did not budge. I knew that if I got into that truck I would probably not be coming back the same. I shouted at the stupid boy as he stood on the sidewalk with both his hands over his useless mouth. He was less than thirty paces from my front door and the thought to run for help had not crossed his mind.

The officer told him to go home. I yelled angrily that I needed him to at the very least skip over to the gate and ring the doorbell before abandoning me. The stupid boy looked at me, mumbled something about how he hoped I would be okay and ran off in the opposite direction from the front door to my house. Realizing I was on my own, I began to scream. This did not please the officer holding the weapon and he raised his gun to my head and told me to shut my mouth. I raised my voice even louder while the officer that had failed at the tasks of shoving my limbs into the car started walking toward the neighbors who were curiously coming out of their homes to find out what was going on. He demanded they turn around because everything was under control and it was a criminal in their custody who was resisting arrest making unnecessary noise. I was still in the midst of a battle royal with the officer who was holding me off the ground and his partner who, despite the growing crowd, still had the barrel of his weapon pressed against my head. It was a fierce struggle but I was able to alert the witnesses that I was not a faceless refugee and that I was in trouble … again.

Negotiations would have been much shorter but for the fact that I kept interjecting and yelling out curses. I was on the ground now and was told by a neighbor to sit quietly in the truck while my family was summoned.

WHERE was my family anyhow?
Were they inside drawing straws to see who had the unfortunate luck of cleaning up the fresh batch of hell I was dishing out?

I knew they could hear me because I could hear the domestic help relaying what was going on outside.

Is this how the boy who cried wolf felt when the beast finally showed up?

Even if I had a tendency to take liberties with the truth, all my past deeds, good or bad, should have fallen to the wayside the moment the house help said, "Gun pointed at her head."

I was busy defiantly screaming that they would have to put my dead bullet-ridden body into the vehicle by the time my family came outside. I do not remember how much money my father had to pay each policeman, but I still remember the disappointed looks from my family, neighbors and even domestic help. Again, I had put myself into harm's way and inconvenienced everybody. After things had calmed down, I thought I would be comforted. Unfortunately, because of my track record nobody bothered. Nobody inquired about my bruises or if I was terribly hurt. It was very frustrating. Almost as infuriating as having to look at the stupid boy the next day and listen to him stumble over an apology.

Life moved on. Trouble came by whenever and however. I came to the United States and he went to the UK. Only two things remained from that day: The occasional pain in my knee and the anger I still have toward the stupid boy who walked away when I needed him most.

.... 11 ....

Driving Miss Daisy.

Victor was such a nice guy. Everybody thought so. His smile left you defenseless and his quiet confidence almost willed you to comply with whatever he requested. His warm and friendly nature elevated the mood of anybody he was around and there seemed to be a lightness and brightness that followed him. He also had the amazing effect of making me more polite, more conscientious, more patient ... just more. That's why it was such a loss that he died.

The only solace I could cling to was believing it would have been more painful had we been a couple, or worse still, if we had been married. That didn't really help. I decided to attend his funeral out of respect for him and offer my condolences to the family that had just lost their son one day after the loss of their father. I could not even try to imagine what they were going through because I was still raw from the recent passing of my own father a few months earlier. Victor's friends in Atlanta were planning to carpool and make the trip to his hometown so I offered to take on a couple of passengers under the assumption that if they knew Victor, we would get along nicely.

Chloe had suggested that we get a hotel room since we were planning to attend both funerals in North Carolina. It would allow us time to offer condolences to Victor's family and close friends, share a meal and return to Atlanta fresh the following day. Made perfect sense – she was so practical, she had to be Victor's friend. In theory it sounded like a great idea. Sadly, I did not do my own calculations to figure out what I was actually signing up for. I would be in a car for eight hours with two strangers, attending two funeral services, sharing dinner with a tableful of strangers, spending the night in the same room with a girl I had been stuck in a car with for eight hours and then driving back to Atlanta with said girl and another passenger for eight hours.

What radio stations do I need to program if they don't like my music? I remember stressing over that more than the air pressure in the tires when driving to pick up my passengers. Chloe had said that she had met Musa at a jazz festival that summer and introduced him to Victor. I didn't have a substantial jazz collection and was looking at my Afro Cuban and Brazilian disc wondering if that would be a good compromise. It was going to have to do because between Nine Inch Nails and Rage Against the Machine, the closest I had to mellow music was The Chemical Brothers. I pulled up to our meeting point and introduced myself to Chloe and Musa and helped load their bags into the truck.

Was he joking when he asked if he could drive my car?

I didn't know him, so I could not gauge his sense of humor but it seemed to me that Musa was sulking in the back seat. I tried to make light of the situation by explaining my insurance rate had just gone up due to a prior collision and under other circumstances I would not hesitate to let a perfect stranger drive my new car. He didn't think that joke was funny. I even put the emphasis on "new" but nothing ... and I think he made a face!

C'mon! In what world does anybody let a stranger drive a new car unless they are in the back seat of a limo?

I decided to leave him to his thoughts and the book he had pulled from his bag and almost ran a red light when I saw the title: The Art of War. This was apparently going to be a long ride. I turned my attention to the road and occasionally glanced over to Chloe when responding to her questions. She was very chatty. I was relieved because I didn't have to worry about the music in the CD changer. She wanted to know what country I was from, how long I had been in the states, what brought me to the States ...

Wait a minute ... what type of Visa? Did she just ask what my immigration status was?

I skipped over that question because I didn't want to get into my usual defensive stance that only Native Americans have the right to this country and we were all foreigners here. My effort to bite my tongue did not escape Musa who immediately pointed to the unanswered question and asked if I was a U.S. citizen or going back to Kenya at some point. Over an hour of debate on who had rights to this country, slavery and civil rights and the detention of undocumented workers, and I was exhausted. We had not even reached Tennessee. Chloe asked if she could turn on the music and I quickly selected the Afro Cuban mix and handed her the jewel case pointing to my favorite tracks that I hoped she might enjoy. As the music played, I mentally calculated how fast I would have to drive to avoid a speeding ticket.

I was very pleasantly surprised when Chloe and Musa emerged from the convenience store with snacks and said they had discussed it and it was only fair that they help out with the gas. I was also glad they had agreed to that before they saw how much gas my SUV could guzzle in a short trip. Salty snacks and carbonated drinks are good tension breakers. Before long, we were having small talk again. Musa was in a better mood, so I attributed his unforgiving spirit to hunger. Chloe was animatedly recollecting her favorite Victor moments. The smile on her face started to fade as she told her last recollection. Her words were shaky. It was understandable. We had lost a good person. I lightly rubbed her shoulder and said that I missed him very much, too. Musa then countered by saying it was such a tragedy since they had made such a lovely couple.

Chloe and Victor a couple?

My chest was constricting and I rolled down the window to allow the wind to rush up my nose because I could feel my lungs forgetting how to process oxygen. I tried to focus on the road while simultaneously playing back the stories she had just told. She had met Victor in May; which was about the same time I met him. Check. She introduced Musa to Victor. Check. She was devoutly religious and enjoyed sharing Bible scripture with Victor. Check. Wait. Was she dating Musa or Victor?

The words couldn't come out of my mouth. I felt like I was drowning slowly in a vat of fudge. I needed to know more but I didn't want to hear anything else. Chloe was thanking Musa and had started sobbing about how unfair life was. I quietly agreed with her 100 percent on that and added a mental note on how cruel fate was. Of all the passengers I could have offered to drive that day, here I was chauffeuring the girl that had won the affection of the man I was madly in love with.

Breathe.

The Carolinas seemed like a continent away. Musa was now telling Chloe that she should take heart because if the circumstances were different she would be a widow. This was too much. My hands were sweaty and I kept wiping them on my jeans in an effort to keep the steering wheel dry. The A/C was on high but I was burning up as my surprise was replaced with anger that was rapidly rising from my core.

Victor had been so considerate when he let me down. I had invited him to a friend's party and he wanted to clarify that we were "just friends" before agreeing to accompany me. Throughout the summer, I had been using social events as an excuse to ask him out and my overt attempts to make us a couple had been noted. He said that while he enjoyed my company and wanted to spend more time with me, he was not ready for a committed relationship and didn't want to lead me on if that was something I hoped for. I reassured him that I was okay with his decision, and that his friendship was all I really wanted. I was crushed but told myself that I would rather have him as a friend than not at all. He was such a great date that night. Everybody loved him and a few girls pulled me aside and said I was crazy if I passively allowed the "friend zone" to control the outcome of what could be a happy union because we were so good together. These girls were right. They had been along for the ride on my other failed attempts at love. Victor was perfect. Made even more attractive because we had never been intimate outside of a hug.

I would look at his mouth as he formed words and wondered how it would be to kiss him. I would watch his hands as he gestured and pictured him holding me. When he wasn't looking I would stare at his body and try to imagine him propped up in bed on a lazy Sunday afternoon quietly allowing me to sketch his features. I imagined our children in the next room playing with soft fluffy toys. I had pictured an entire life with him.

"Get the hell out of my car!" is what I wanted to scream at this stranger who had magically transformed into a mortal enemy. I wanted to pull over and yank her out of the seat. Her and her horrible sidekick Musa. Her and her perfect cheekbones. Her and her melodic little girlie voice. Her and her lovely long hair. Her and her slender toned body. Her and her vegetarian, recycling, church going, volunteering ass needed to get out of my life immediately.

THIS is what Victor picked over me? Why her? I let the tears roll down my face knowing I already had an excuse to be sad and crying at that moment. Then it occurred to me that Chloe would think I was crying over HER loss and my tears immediately dried up.

My anger was stronger than my self-pity. I turned my attention to the conversations I had previously had with the man of my dreams. When Victor said that he wasn't ready for a relationship, did he stop the sentence short? Did he mean to say he wasn't ready for a relationship ... with me? When he made scripture references, was that an indication that I had not made the spiritual grade? He was in the gym everyday and would joke about what I ate, was that another red flag that my short and pudgy body didn't measure up with this skinny, tall, athletic heifer over here weeping ever so politely into her embroidered handkerchief?

I hadn't realized how fast I was apparently driving until a voice in the backseat mocked that two funerals that day was plenty. How big was South Carolina anyhow? My truck felt tiny traveling down on this endless road and its interior felt even smaller. There wasn't enough room for my anger and the hostility being rained down on me from Musa's attacks and there definitely was not enough room to accommodate Chloe's now larger than life immaculate Madonna status.

If I crash this car just right, there is a high chance I might be the sole survivor.

Anger usually sways my decisions, but pessimism and sarcasm have the last word. I thought about the smiling faces of my family and friends whenever I talked about Victor. I wasn't about to bring them pain. Not over a man who had made a terrible mistake. That's what this was; a horrible error that could never be corrected. It wasn't Chloe's fault that Victor didn't live long enough to know better and had picked the wrong girl. Poor Victor. Poor Chloe. I was feeling a little better.

I heard it said that you can always tell the kind of impact a person has had in life by the number of mourners that show up for the funeral. Victor and his dad were wonderful people. The little town was overwhelmed by the amount of traffic going through it. Every other car tag was out of state. Louisiana, Mississippi, Washington D.C. and Virginia. It was tragically beautiful to behold. Victor's childhood friends welcomed us warmly.

What the hell did this guy mean, "We have heard all about you"?

He had Chloe's wrist tucked under his arm and was introducing her saying "THIS is Chloe" and that would be followed by acknowledged sighs, tight hugs and sympathetic nods. This was a terrible, terrible mistake. Where was my preamble? Had he never mentioned me to his friends? How about a co-worker? Distant cousin? No? I was in a terrible state. I was imploding where I stood and trying hard to focus on why I was there. This was not about Chloe anymore. I had to make the decision if I wanted to join the line viewing the recently departed. I had to express my condolences to his family and friends. I had to say goodbye.

It was impossible not to cry. I went through my entire box of tissue and now one of Victor's close friends was trying to comfort me in the pew. Self-pity, anger and loss are a terrible and potent combination. I had become a stereotype, the mourner who weeps louder than the family. After the service I thought I had composed myself adequately enough to meet Victor's mother and brothers. But I was incoherent. Again I was being comforted by the family of the deceased. Thankfully, I heard Chloe's angelic voice behind me and my rage returned and quickly mopped up the tears.

For the remainder of the day, I used her. Chloe became my reset button when I felt the tears well up or my lip begin to tremble. To numb the pain I would glare at her and make tiny catty observations to myself and the audience in my head:

Look at this one over here ordering drinks. I don't remember a "tequila and lime with sugar on the rim" scripture the last time I was in church ... and granted it has been a while, but I don't think THAT much has changed.

Speech? Who the heck does she think she is? This heifer here thinks she is Jackie O or something, right? She's not family. She will never be family now, so she needs to sit the hell back down and lick her glass if she needs something to do with that mouth.

Dancing? Hypocrite! Go ahead and go shake a leg in a nightclub and pretend that is part of the wake -- like nobody else saw Musa's hand around your waist.

THIS is what he picked over me? Her? This girl over here?!

Morning could not come fast enough. While Musa and Chloe were loading up their bags, I made slight adjustments to the music options. I wasn't about to accommodate either of them any longer so the ride back was going to be very fast, extremely loud and hopefully painful for them.

Nine Inch Nails. Check.
System of a Down. Disturbed. Check and check.
Strap in. Enjoy the Chop Suey and get Down With The Sickness. Bitches.

.... 12 ....

Was that wrong? Really?

The idea that we have to teach children to be good suggests that the human condition, by default, wants to be bad. What exactly is "bad" anyway and who gets to decide when societal norms change over time? Maybe the transgression we are committing today is just ahead of the collective value system? No? If you aren't onboard with that, then this story will be a little difficult for me to defend. Particularly since it happened 20 years ago.

I had a regular childhood. Regular in that it was similar to that of my friends and relatives. Rode bicycles around the neighborhood. Climbed trees. Had chickens for pets. Slapped a teacher in first grade. Well, maybe not so regular in some respects. I did spent a lot of time in detention ... evil nuns took such pleasure in punishing me. Lucky for me my parents were not big on corporal punishment, regardless of the deed. My parents were also very supportive of my sisters and me growing up. It helped that we were smart girls and in our house, clever trumped naughty every time. So I got away with quite a bit.

Her name was Lina and I went home and told my father that I had a crush on her. There was no fear, or shame, or awkwardness in sharing this information. My father was not angry. He joked about having me for a son and told me it was okay to like a girl, but since I might change my mind when I grew up, we would hold off turning me into a boy as I had requested. We were in Africa. I was 10 years old at the time. I took his and my mother's acceptance for granted and it wasn't until I was living in the United States and heard stories about how teens were kicked out of their homes, or forced to run away from their families, that I realized how fortunate I was. This story is not about Lina. It is about the one who followed her five years later. The girl that was my awakening.

Kristen was never on time. She always apologized for keeping me waiting. I was sitting on the edge of her bed and she promised that she would take less than ten minutes to be out of the bathroom, and that we'd be heading out the door in less than 15. True to her word, she was quick in the shower and walked back into her bedroom with a towel loosely tied around her wet body.

We were in an all-girls primary school and on occasion we saw each other naked when changing for swimming lessons. Kristen was comfortable being nude around other girls and blissfully unaware that I was not a regular classmate. I was pretending to be engrossed in the fashion magazines she had stacked on the bed to keep me occupied while I waited. I was watching her dry off. I flipped the pages of the magazine and read aloud to her to suggest that I was interested in what a particular celebrity was wearing. Instead I was intently watching as she applied lotion on her legs and then her thighs. She had flawless skin and I wanted to touch every inch of it. She was asking me to grab a bra from the chest of drawers next to her bed. I couldn't take my eyes off her breasts. So delicate. Mine were much larger and I wondered how hers would feel to the touch. I asked her if I picked hers or her sister's bra by mistake (as an excuse to keep staring at her chest) while I pretended that the item I had in my hands was much too big. This inevitably led into a conversation about body image and Kristen was now standing in front of a full length mirror pointing out the parts of her perfect body that she wanted to change. I stood beside her pretending to critique her upper arms and thighs and butt - all the while engraving every detail into my memory.

Lotion never smelled so good. We used the exact same product but on her it took on a totally different characteristic. I was so close to her. The awareness that I could reach out and caress her was making me dizzy. Or maybe it was because I was holding my breath for fear that I had breathed in too deeply one too many times. I was also a little embarrassed that I was having this experience at her expense and was doing everything in my power to prolong it.

There were no secrets between my parents and me as I was growing up. My mother and father knew about the first time I got drunk (it was a school night). The first time I smoked marijuana (I called my mother in a panic because I thought I was dying). I told them everything. Good or bad. Including that time when those evil nuns said I was possessed by the devil to explain why I would keep fainting in church (low blood sugar … Satan shouldn't be blamed for everything). This however, I kept to myself. I didn't tell a soul.

I went to a different secondary school, so the only time I was able to see Kristen was over the weekend. It was quite a commitment. I would walk for 10 minutes to the closest bus stop. After a 20-minute commute into the city, I would walk about 20 more minutes across town to catch the bus that went by Kristen's area. The walk from that bus stop to Kristen's neighborhood was a good half hour. I always timed it so I would be much earlier than we had planned because I knew it meant she wasn't ready. I wasn't always lucky, but on the days I caught her exiting the shower, it was well worth the trouble.

My father was right. As time passed, my attention shifted to boys. While I have never truly lost interest in women, I do know that I want to eventually settle down and marry a man and start a family. There are times though when I have to pause. When a woman leans in front of me and I find myself looking down her blouse, or when I find myself calculating exactly when to glance up a woman's skirt while she is crossing her legs. That's when I have to wonder if I have been forcefully teaching myself to be with men when my nature suggests otherwise.

.... 13 ....

Let me get this straight ... you want our future kids to worship whom?

God bless my mother and the hell I put her through. My parents, like most others, played "good cop, bad cop," and in our house mum was the disciplinarian. I don't remember if there was an unspoken agreement among the kids, but I was cast in the role of "unruly prisoner number 3" for most of the drama that unfolded in our family. I took my responsibilities very seriously and tested my mother's resolve at every turn. Partly because I was a brat, but mostly because, while she did a ton of scolding, our mother did not believe in severe spanking. The most physical she ever got was a tiny pinch on our inner thigh. That's it. I wasn't afraid of a tiny pinch so I would challenge her, talk back and was just a terror. There was one time she was so enraged that she said I was the devil spawn. I turned my thirteen-year-old insolent face to her and said that she must have been sleeping with Satan if that was the case. Tiny pinch, a few days of good behavior as penance, and I was back to my wicked ways.

That is why it caught me so off-guard a few years ago when I had this incredible need to have a baby. In the past, I was always quick to check off the box "single, no children, thank you" and would go as far as eliminating a potential male candidate when dating because I did not want to become an instant mother to his children. It is not that I don't like children. I love, love being an aunty. I make an AWESOME aunty. It is the tiny videotape that looped in my head replaying all the terrible things I said and did to my mother growing up that put my body in a state of panic when I imagined my own daughter pulling off half the stunts I did. What kind of hypocrite would I be for pointing out the speck of dirt in my child's eye, when earthmovers couldn't keep up with the gravel pouring out of mine? I was so determined not to have children that at seventeen I went to have my tubes tied. Didn't happen. Parental approval got in the way. Plus, the doctor, his staff and the people in the waiting room were laughing so hard, I'm not sure the surgery would have gone well.

Pregnancy really got in the way of my enjoying sex as a young adult. That, plus I wasn't really into boys. There were times I wondered if I chased after girls to run away from the risk of being impregnated. Could my fear of having a tiny me be that strong? Whatever the case, the council of elders in my head agreed that no child would pass through my loins. The motion was passed and I thought I was onboard until out of nowhere a new videotape began to play in my head.

It was a sinister video. There I was breastfeeding and rocking a baby to sleep. There I sat helping my little one tie a shoelace. Oh look, I am baking! I can bake? All these fake imaginings about how perfect my life would be, if only I had a baby, aggressively took over my head. This video had powerful allies in the form of awareness. Everywhere I turned, friends were having babies. My siblings were having babies. I was bumping into pregnant women. Every movie on TV was about women trying to have babies or announcing happily that they were pregnant. An emergency session was called to oust the video running rampant in my thoughts. But to my surprise, the elders had lost their conviction. Words like "maybe" and "if" had replaced "no" and a new constitution was being drafted by my brain as I realized in horror that I had less than four years to find a suitable man to fall madly in love with, get married and get pregnant (at least twice) before the window of opportunity closed.

God bless the Internet. God bless Internet dating sites and instant messaging and smart phones. I was only a few clicks away from warm baby breath and I channeled all my energy toward this new goal. The same commitment my mother had witnessed in my defiant behavior was unleashed onto three dating sites simultaneously. I was casting for the role of future baby daddy.

Every checkbox when filling out my profile became more important than sitting for the SAT. Height. Weight. Physical fitness. Smoking or not. Social drinking: how many is a few? Political views. Religion. Interests. The only thing that was not a deal breaker was profession. I have met some doctors and lawyers who are real jerks and some really nice blue-collar guys, so occupation was not at the top of my list; race was. I shouldn't have to defend that one. I am black. I would like a black baby with thick tangled unmanageable hair like mine. Besides, I don't think there is a group of 30-something Caucasian or Asian women sitting around discussing if they should keep their options open and date outside their race. I get upset when talking to my girlfriends and hear that apparently I have to give up on my preference. To avoid the whole black/white thing, I restricted myself to only checking African American and setting that preference as "very important." It seemed a little redundant since the sites had names like Black People or Black Planet or something with "black" in there.

That's why it was such a surprise when he showed up white.

Daniel and I hit it off from the first moment I responded to his invitation to connect. He was funny. Very important. Smart without being obnoxious. Very important. Had traveled extensively, including trips to Ghana, Mali, Togo, Ivory Coast and a host of other African countries that I had only learned about in school or caught glimpses of on the Discovery Channel. He loved to cook. He loved his family. He did not go to church. All excellent qualities. Particularly the last one (I was finding it challenging to meet men who couldn't get past my not being a member of a church or attending services regularly). We had been communicating for a couple of weeks. First email, then instant messaging and eventually working up to phone calls. He had a great voice. Our first date was set and I looked at the black-and-white photo on his profile hoping the reason he had a baseball cap on was that he was a big fan of the Atlanta Braves and not due to a receding hairline.

I heard my name come out of his mouth. I was walking toward the smiling man, with a full head of blonde hair, while having an out-of-body experience. With every step closer, I thought back to his profile. Did I make a mistake? Did he check the wrong box? What about all the discussions about the motherland? Do white people refer to Africa as the motherland now? He didn't seem to have even the tiniest hint of a tan despite the fact that it was August. Maybe he is a very, very light-skinned black man? I couldn't tell. I couldn't ask. So we had lunch. It was great. We laughed and talked like old friends. The only awkward pause occurred when he invited me back to his house to watch a DVD that we had discussed. After sending a friend a text with his name and address, I followed him home.

Again with the Africa stuff. Masks from Cameroon on the walls. Ugandan currency on display under the glass topped coffee table. I couldn't ask. He pulled out the photo album and was flipping through photos of him in Accra visiting his sister and brother-in-law. His sister looked so pale in comparison to the statuesque African man beside her. I couldn't tell. Daniel made no mention about the obvious contrast in hue in the photo that was quietly mocking me and daring me to ask. I was so tense. I was desperate to log onto a computer to get to the bottom of this puzzle. Did he check black or white? Did it matter? Apparently, it did because even when I saw the African-American box clearly checked, I made flimsy excuses when he would call to ask me out again. Daniel lost interest while I had moved on and was busy connecting with Jaheim. This time I made sure to look at all the photos. What a fine specimen Jaheim was. We would make beautiful babies.

Jaheim lived alone. He had never been married or had any children, but wanted to settle down and start a family. Great. He was flattered that I wanted to meet after only three short phone conversations. I told him that it would be best if we both put all our cards on the table and talked about our expectations so that if our goals were not the same, we'd save some time. He said that he liked my direct, no nonsense approach. He wasn't aware that this was not a date … this was an interview. Before our meeting, I studied his profile and read through all the emails we had exchanged. There were not going to be any surprises. He looked better in real life. Beautiful black man. I didn't recall a speech impediment when we had spoken on the phone, but Jaheim seemed to be having trouble forming words.

I was apologizing for the loud music and confessing that I was having some difficulty hearing him, when Jaheim made a confession of his own. He was a little drunk. Now, I am not prudish about many things and I have often given people the benefit of a doubt (usually to my own detriment), but showing up to a first date intoxicated? Jaheim had the perfect explanation: I had pushed our date back one hour so he had a little time on his hands and thought a couple of drinks would calm his nerves. That was sweet. He was nervous about meeting me. However, men who cannot handle their alcohol are as unattractive to me as a person breaking wind in a crowded elevator. I conferred with the advisors in my head and we agreed that we would temporarily defer the lapse in judgment for future review and move on to more pressing matters.

Me too. Me too! Despite the slurring that got less noticeable as I started to drink, Jaheim and I were clicking very nicely. Outside of the things we had checked off on our profiles and discussed online, we had similar interests and our social lives in Atlanta seemed to be parallel. We had stumbled onto the topic of museums because I had recently attended a Van Gogh exhibit and we were discussing museums in different cities we had visited. Jaheim had just finished talking about the exhibit that was on its way to Atlanta which he had seen on his last trip to Washington D.C.. I was looking forward to that Pharaoh exhibit. As I was rattling away, Jaheim was busy rolling up the sleeve of his shirt to proudly display his tattoo. It was huge and had a lot going on. There was an eye, a pyramid and hieroglyphic characters and a falcon or maybe it was an eagle. I wasn't looking at the tattoo as much as I was admiring the muscular arm it adorned.

That's when the conversation took a sudden turn.

I was now focusing hard on Jaheim to make sure I fully comprehended what he was saying. It had to be the alcohol. This beautiful, seemingly normal man was telling me that he was a direct descendent of the sun god. He had done the research and all Africans at one time were one nation under Ra until the white man came and brainwashed us with Christianity. He said that it was our responsibility to take our true religion back. At that point he loudly spouted out Osiris, Amun, Anubis and a host of other ancient deities I had left behind in my history books, while I looked around uncomfortably hoping that the people seated closest to us could not hear our conversation. He proclaimed that the tattoo gave him a spiritual connection to his ancestral line and it was his charge to raise his children as true believers.

He had to be pulling my leg. I kept smiling thinking that at any moment he was going to say "gotcha" and we'd laugh about how funny he was. The moment was taking its time to come so I decided to play along. I asked Jaheim if he had ever lived in Egypt. He had not. He didn't even have a passport. My beautiful specimen went on to say that it wasn't necessary to go to Africa because he had researched online and found a commune that practiced the ancient way right here in good ol' USA. Perfect. Africa ... without the inconvenience of Africans. I did not make any polite excuses about calling him the next day, or ever again.

The decision-makers in my head agreed to my request to review the progress to date. After Daniel and Jaheim came the masseur who promised that giving me a full body massage would not be sexual ... at all! After him was the data analyst who grew out his nails on his left hand and would never look me in the face when he spoke. After him came the widower who had just buried his wife of seven years that previous month and spent our date trying to figure out what kind of sick and desperate woman would be okay with stepping into his late wife's shoes so quickly. After him ...

It was enough. I had made my case and bought a year's worth of silence and resumed my sole role as world's best aunty.

······· 14 ·······

I should have earned Skymiles for that.

He had asked me to marry him over the phone. Not very romantic. Especially because that was his way to end the heated argument we were having. This was just like Nick; he was the type of person who instead of replacing old furniture, wanted to buy a new house in order to start fresh. Our relationship had so many challenges. The least of which was the distance between us. I had not seen him in one year but we talked frequently. The current disagreement was about my astronomical phone bill, which I said was evidence that I DID love him. Nick was not convinced and said that if I truly loved him, I would fly to London for a visit. I replied that his suggestion was illogical and that he only wanted sex and I wished he would just be honest for once. He countered with a marriage proposal to shut me up. I did not like that at all. It was not genuine and I was so offended and tired of his passive aggressive nonsense that I wanted to break up that instant. Instead I told Nick that I was going to visit after all so I could give him my answer to his face.

It was November 2000. Long before anybody knew what TSA was. Long before secondary screening and three fluid ounces and all the new rituals that come with air travel today. The airport screener was going through my carry-on luggage to retrieve the set of handcuffs that had shown up on the x-ray. She pushed aside the feather boa, the whip and all the leather and lace lingerie that I had purchased earlier that week and summoned a supervisor to view the entire contents of the case. Other passengers were looking as one-by-one they pulled out the neatly folded angel wings (made from real feathers) and an assortment of adult novelty toys.

The supervisor asked why I had not packed these "goodies" into my checked luggage and I explained that I lost luggage on a previous flight and didn't want to repeat that experience. She then held the handcuffs up and said that I could not legally carry them onto a plane. I quickly showed how they worked by pointing out the safety release and explained the item was not real. A small crowd of security screeners were collecting around my bags so I decided to do what I did when I was uncomfortable ... go for shock value. I loudly declared that I was an exotic dancer and I was paid in advance to attend a bachelor party in London and I needed the cuffs and all my props (including the vibrator that was now being tested) for the show. That seemed to satisfy the supervisor who began helping me pack my belongings back, with the exception of the handcuffs that I was told would be waiting at security on my return. I bid farewell to the group of screeners and smiled brightly as they wished me the best of luck and a successful night complete with piles of money.

I couldn't focus on the in-flight entertainment. I was still upset over the loss of a very expensive set of handcuffs. Nick was going to have to pay for that. I went over my plan:

1. Pretend I am really happy to see him.
2. Use the props and toys to have all the deviant sex I could dream up.
3. Get a nice tour of London town.
4. Say "absolutely not" to his proposal and break up with him.
5. Fly back to Atlanta.

Did he just call me chubby?

I was standing in Nick's living room wearing a black vinyl leotard with silver claps and zippers all over the place. I looked down at myself and at the black boots and my grasp tightened on the whip in my hand and I glared back at Nick. Yes I had gained some weight since I last saw him but that was irrelevant. I looked good and more importantly I looked like I was ready for some hardcore action. Bastard. He was making the whole "pretend to be happy" a lot harder than it needed to be. I was going to need some help. Luckily, Nick had stocked the kitchen shelves with a lot of alcohol and I had packed a tube of lubricant. It was going to be a long night.

Nick was apologizing the following morning over breakfast that he would not be able to take me into town to show me around because he had to work. More nonsense. He knew my itinerary and the duration of my trip. I asked which days he got off and almost stabbed him in the face when he replied that he had not requested any days off. He reassured me that we would have plenty of time together … at night. I held back a scream. This was not going according to plan. I was going to have to turn on the charm and slather him with sex that night. I needed to leave him crushed and broken in five days and didn't have time to spare. I was also not going to waste my time in his nasty apartment so I asked for a map and some instructions for the train and proceeded to take myself into the city.

London in November was dismal. I was irritated at The Tate and didn't want to pretend to be as deeply immersed as all the students around me so I left. I couldn't get anybody to volunteer to take my photo at Tower Bridge and that darkened my day even more. The only highlight was getting a ticket for a production of Cats, but I was so exhausted from walking around all day, that I fell asleep and missed the majority of the show. That was a very expensive nap. Nick was going to pay for that too. On the train ride back to Nick's I realized that I was wasting a golden opportunity. I wasn't breaking up with London, it was Nick that I was mad at. I made a pact between myself and the city to enjoy the rest of my sightseeing despite my reason for being there.

Red boa. Lacy, little frilly camisole with matching strips of ribbon masquerading as a thong. On. I looked very hot. Why was I so itchy? Was it a reaction to the fabric? Was my body physically rejecting the very idea of having another night of pretend love-making? Morning seemed so far away.

Nick was smiling as he filled the tub for me to sit in and cool off from the full-blown yeast infection I had woken up with. He said that it was my punishment for applying cheap flavored and scented lubricant. He went off to work leaving me in the windowless bathroom staring at cracks in the tile as I revised my plan:

1. Find a pharmacist.
2. Enjoy sights to get my mind off irritating itch.
3. End things with Nick.

London was not co-operating. Either the whole city was conspiring against me, or the conveniences I took for granted in Atlanta were unparalleled.

Where is the pharmacy? Ok, chemist. Where is the chemist? Why do I have to explain again what a yeast infection is? Are there no females in London who ever get a yeast infection? HOW MUCH for that pill and where is the accompanying cream hiding? I need that cream! No, yogurt is not "just as good and better for me," you clowns.

What kind of hell is this?

I had walked too long outdoors in bad weather. By the time I returned to Nick's apartment, the itch was a burn, my feet were numb, my back was hurting and I was sniffling. There was no way I was going to let my body suffer this much in an attempt to potentially hurt his ego. There was also no guarantee that he would be hurt, so why stick around pretending London was wonderful? I edited my plan of action accordingly as I walked to the bathroom with a cupful of yogurt.

1. Break up immediately.
2. Change plane ticket.
3. Change home phone number.

Is he crying?

Nick had been ambushed by my foul mood. The insults I was hurling gained in strength and number as I perceived chinks in his amour. Nothing was spared. I attacked his character. I went after his family and friends. I attacked his dwelling. I even attacked his city for inefficient access to pharmaceuticals.

I was shifting uneasily in my seat going over what I had thought was a foolproof plan when I was purchasing my plane ticket. The medication was not working and neither was the home remedy. I should have ended things over the phone. This was going to be a long flight home.

.... 15 ....

Wounded Deer.

My roommate had a name for the first girl I had oral sex with. He referred to her as The Wounded Deer because of all the preparation, planning, stalking and eventual dispatching of "the prey" during my sophomore year in college. I could tell she was nervous being around me. Becky was confident, energetic and eager to participate in group work, but when it came to speaking with me one-on-one, she turned into a mumbling, sheepish, awkward mess. It was perfect. I knew exactly what she was feeling and precisely how to proceed with her.

I had witnessed firsthand how Eddy handled his women. There was always a woman in queue waiting for her chance to date him despite the fact that he did not treat them very nicely. That seemed to be the secret of his success. I asked Eddy what kind of drug he was administering to keep these crazy girls coming back for more. He pointed out that he found it interesting for me to be asking that question, considering that I was folding his laundry as we spoke. I looked down at the neatly stacked jeans and socks rolled up (just the way he liked) and realized that I was a rank and file member of his squad. How did it happen? How was he able to recruit me, happily nested in the middle of my ultra-lesbian "death to men" army, to unwittingly do his bidding? I was not angry. I was impressed and fascinated, and now highly motivated to learn what I could.

The training grounds consisted of the student center on campus and a small university-friendly neighborhood bar. I would get Eddy food and drinks and he would share nuggets of wisdom and demonstrate how to apply his technique. It was amazing to watch what I thought was a load of crap actually work each and every time. For Becky, he suggested a sure fire method that he used very sparingly. Eddy said that he would open up to a woman in his friendly and charismatic way and then without warning share something very personal and intimate. He would then apologize and withdraw and become evasive. That was the most stupid game plan I had ever heard so I pressed him to elaborate further. He explained that he believed that human beings barter emotion. If he shared a compromising piece of information about himself and did not appear to want the recipient of the information to reciprocate in kind, there would be an imbalance in that interaction. The recipient of that fragile bit of himself would then feel the need to be vulnerable and open herself to him and give more than she ever planned. I was intrigued. I felt nothing for Becky so it would be easy to evaluate the success of the method.

A mumbling Becky was thanking me for volunteering to present our group's findings to the entire class. I told her it was the least I could do considering how unpleasantly I had treated her. Becky looked confused. I went on to apologize and said that ever since she had colored her hair and cropped it short, she looked like my ex-girlfriend. I took the liberty to lightly stroke the hairline closest to her ear and watched a very uncomfortable Becky catch her breath as I explained how my emotions were all over the place and it was wrong for me to vent my frustrations on her. I recognized that I was not following Eddy's exact method. I didn't have his outgoing personality and funny sense of humor so I modified my approach, but ensured an equal trade would not occur. Becky was trying to confess that she, too, was struggling with feelings toward me. I cut her off before she could say anything else. I apologized profusely again and said I would try to stop staring at her because I was sure it was making her uncomfortable. Then I rushed out of the room.

Eddy said my phone rung almost every hour while I was working my evening shift. We both had sinister smiles on our faces as we sipped beers and replayed Becky's voicemail. Eddy complimented me on the hair touch and suggested that on my next encounter I should show that I was struggling to restrain myself from making physical contact with her body and mimic some of her awkwardness to indicate that SHE was the one making me nervous. Diabolical.

Nothing short of genius. I was happily cooking Eddy dinner while relating the success of the day's events and toasting his future Nobel Prize-winning mind. Becky was nervous and excited. She was unsure of herself and how to interact with me. Again, I offered profuse apologies for my behavior and blamed it on my attraction to women that looked like her and quickly made my exit leaving all my emotional trinkets with her and taking nothing in exchange. The class met on Monday and Wednesday. Under Eddy's instruction, I was to miss the upcoming class and not communicate with Becky until the following Monday. The evasive period was upon us.

Voicemail number one was light and friendly. I wondered how long Becky had practiced sounding nonchalant before calling to casually check in on me. Voicemail number two the following day betrayed some strain as Becky was offering to bring her notes from the last lecture if I needed them. On Saturday, a concerned Becky called and detailed her weekend plans so I could know when and where to catch her. I was tempted to call. I was sure she was getting irritated. Eddy instructed otherwise and laid out the plan.

I walked up to Becky as she was getting settled for the lecture and ask if we could talk someplace private that evening. She agreed to meet me at the park. We walked in silence and I led her off the biking trail to a more secluded area. I did not say a word. Eddy had been adamant on that point. We reached a little stone bench and I sat down and looked at the ground. Becky began her confession.

Eddy was right. Becky shared her fears that her attraction and feelings toward me would not be welcome and wanted to know what she could do to make me comfortable. She promised that she would never hurt me and proclaimed how she was ready to be with somebody she could truly connect with and she knew that I was the one. Eddy knew his women. Per his instructions, I interrupted Becky with a light kiss. And then a deeper more intense kiss complete with hesitant hand movements all along her face and back. I felt ridiculous, but it was working. Becky was responding in kind and hurriedly trying to unfasten my belt buckle. It was time to retreat again. I made an excuse about the time and asked if I could see her over the weekend. She agreed.

Drinks were on me. Eddy was surveying the new faces at the bar while explaining that I had nothing else to do but sit back and enjoy the ride. It didn't matter what I said at this point, Becky knew I was interested and thought I was vulnerable and was going to go out of her way to meet me halfway. He was right. The previously nervous Becky transformed into a very eager and willing participant for any suggestion I came up with. I had never satisfied a woman orally before and now thanks to Becky I was getting all the practice I wanted. It was now time to put all my acquired skill to use on a girl who I was actually interested in. I consulted Eddy on how to disengage from my now unnecessary situation.

My instructions had been clear. I failed to follow them. I thought I could modify Eddy's method of being aloof and chronically unavailable, by simply not communicating with Becky at all. The semester was over and I thought the summer break would be enough of a buffer. The phone calls and angry voicemails turned into furious pounding at the front door.

Eddy and I stood outside our apartment two weeks later reading the obscene message that had defaced our front door. He said it was Becky. I said it was one of his women, most likely the one who had keyed the entire length of his car.

.... 16 ....

His name was "Cornbread." (Note to self: Never mess around with a grown man who still uses nicknames).

"For Sistas Only" was in its second year in Atlanta. We heard on the radio that it was THE place to be if you were female, black and single. I was planning to get natural hair products for my dreadlocks and see if I could track down a particular incense brand that had eluded me in all the stores where I was hunting it down. Khadijah was excited about going because she had picked out a beautiful ring the year before and was hoping to add it to her jewelry collection. She did not have a cell phone so we made plans to meet at the agreed-upon vendor booth every hour to check in, until we were ready to leave.

First check in, and we were both in high spirits. I had found my incense and she was sporting a chunky rock with intricate metalwork that extended the length of her middle finger. Khadijah had stopped walking and squeezed my wrist with her free hand. I glanced up from admiring her ring to find she was smiling and looking ahead of us. I turned my head and saw him standing directly in our path and staring unapologetically at us. Khadijah was letting out a nervous giggle as the man was making his way very deliberately through the milling crowd toward us. I felt my face involuntarily break out into a wide smile. Neither of us could help it. He was gorgeous. I loved that about our excursions into Atlanta from our Cobb County suburbs; everywhere you turned there were beautiful black men. We were trying to speak without moving our lips and only managed a few excited exclamations before our beautiful Atlanta specimen was within reach. He even smelled beautiful. Musky and manly and bold.

He extended his arm to introduce himself to Khadijah. I knew the drill. I would smile politely as he greeted me and then as the focus shifted back to my friend, I would make a flimsy excuse to leave and allow the furious flirting to commence. It wasn't Khadijah's fault. She was extremely beautiful and men would very often find themselves stumbling over the right words to say to hold her attention for a brief moment. There had even been a few occasions where men would talk to me to find out how to get closer to her. I didn't mind because it usually meant not having to worry about the cover charge to whatever club we were accosted in front of, or lots of free drinks once we got inside.

I was only half paying attention as he asked my name because I was trying to figure out how I would occupy myself for the next hour while the two beautiful people next to me embarked on the flawlessly executed temptress dance they were both so well versed in. I saw a vendor booth for Afrocentric attire and announced to Khadijah that I was going to try on some dresses and would meet her at our check in spot in about an hour. I shook the beautiful man's hand as he (like so many other men) inquired if I should really be leaving so quickly. The other guys were always betrayed by their sly smiles but this guy was something else. He was trying too hard. So concerned about my departure. So ridiculous about asking when we could meet again. We all knew I was the third wheel so why prolong the inevitable? Khadijah intervened and steered him away in the opposite direction and I proceeded to the stack of pretty fabrics that would be my refuge for the next forty-five minutes.

My cell phone ringing always caught me off guard because it was a time when pagers were still widely in use and my phone was usually only for emergencies. I did not recognize the voice on the other end and could only make out a few words because the Georgia World Congress Center, which housed the annual event, was now packed and very loud. It was him. What was going on? Where was Khadijah? Why was he telling me to turn around? I looked over my shoulder and there he was. Standing perfectly still again, and staring intently with his cell phone up to his ear.

He was still talking as he casually walked toward me and I hurriedly explained that his call was costing me a fortune so I was hanging up. He was smiling but I was not. Where was my friend and what had he done to prompt her to give him my number? He was explaining that Khadijah had gone to grab a bite to eat to allow us to get to know each other a little better. How irritating. I loved Khadijah but I was not planning to spend that afternoon as her emissary and play nice with this guy. I knew the type. Soften up the girlfriends and family as a way to get himself entrenched. Apparently my disdain had made its way to my face because he was now apologizing for approaching me since it was obvious I was not interested in him. My confused expression was countered by amusement, followed by relief on his. He quickly clarified it was me he was trying to talk to and not Khadijah.

This was a twist that I did not see coming. Now that he had expelled my assumptions, he proceeded to introduce himself again. I was listening this time and smiled manically when he told me to call him Cornbread.

Poetry night and our first official date. Cornbread led me into the dimly lit café that was hosting the open mic session. I felt like I was in a scene from a movie as he whipped out his little notebook and sauntered to the stage. I wasn't even paying attention to his poem; I was basking in the glow of all the envious single women who were trying to casually turn their heads to see why his eyes were not fixed on them as he read out loud. I knew they were sizing me up. He was a very good-looking man and in comparison to him I was a solid 7 ... 8.5 with makeup. I smiled politely back at a table of 9s and 10s as Cornbread made his way back to his seat. The smile quickly faded as the pain shot up from my toes that were trapped under the weight of his shoe. He apologized profusely and wanted to inspect the damage himself by rubbing lightly and examining my foot for any sign of broken skin. He then placed both my legs into his lap and began to massage my feet to the apparent horror of a few 10s. It must have too much for them to contend with. My smile was back and it never left my face for the entire evening.

Cornbread lived in a very eclectic part of the city where old factories had been converted into upscale and exclusive condos. He gave me the grand tour that city dwelling people seem obliged to give suburbanites. The view from the windows was spectacular, but I could not justify ever paying the amount of rent he did for the little space he got in return. The area set aside for his sleeping quarters was so tiny that only a twin size bed could fit in the sectioned off portion of the space. I did love the floors. Every place I had ever lived had carpet, but he had cool-to-the-touch smooth concrete floors that I was enjoying walking on barefoot. On an entire wall he had sketches of dresses taped up beside a full-length mirror. Color swatches and fabric samples were pinned to a corkboard alongside little scribbled notes with various women's names and sizes. There was a wireframe mannequin rising up from yards of cloth piled on the floor and a solid box on a table that I assumed held a sewing machine. He wasn't joking when he said he designed women's clothes on the day we met.

He was also quite serious when he requested that I disrobe and try on a dress he needed to make adjustments on. I snorted at this because my 5'2" frame had never been mistaken for that of a model. Cornbread walked to his shoebox-sized bedroom to fetch the dress as I stood looking at the full-length mirror with a decision to make.

I regretted my choice of underwear and made a mental note to invest in a few decent bras because this was not a pretty picture. All my exposed skin was covered in goose bumps as Cornbread helped me into a dress that was cut for a woman with a smaller chest, smaller hips and much longer legs than mine. My disillusionment was trying to pitch a fit and argued that it was his plan to get me naked and all the fashion stuff was just a clever smoke screen to further that scheme. Cornbread must have sensed the impending uprising in my head because he went on to explain that he had two of the exact same garment and mistakenly grabbed the smaller one. Minutes later I was admiring a perfectly fitting gown. Cornbread was complementing my body and then himself because the only adjustment necessary was taking the hem up by three inches. I didn't want to take it off. It was like second skin and I felt like a 10.

Something definitely felt different. I was pushing an exhausted Cornbread off me and he almost toppled out of the bed. Twin beds are not built for two. As he stood naked in front of me I saw what was missing. The condom. I watched him put it on. Where was it now? He was smiling and telling me not to worry. I was frantically explaining that I was not on a safe day and having a prophylactic lodged inside me was a mini disaster. The situation did not call for calm and his responses were in such stark contrast to what I was expecting that it awoke my paranoia. Something was very wrong.

I asked him quietly because I didn't want to hear his response. Cornbread said "yes" without hesitation. I then asked why he had slipped off the condom and his reply was "because you looked clean."

The one thing I love about the suburbs is the hospitals. So efficient and inviting and quiet, even on a Saturday at 3 a.m. The receiving nurse read my intake form and within fifteen minutes I was in an exam room with a doctor, nurse and rape counselor. I knew it was wrong to take up their time with my tall tale about being at a nightclub and waking up in the backseat of a stranger's car with my underwear around my ankles. Somewhere a real rape victim had to relate the horror of what had just occurred to her and here I was; reclined on an exam table pretending to be shell shocked in an effort to ensure that no pregnancy would result from Cornbread's stupidity.

My credit card bill came and I looked at the line item showing the charge for the emergency room visit. It was the most expensive birth control pill I had ever purchased. Khadijah said it was unwise to ever contact him again, but I was adamant about the cost being shared. Cornbread answered the phone and asked me to remind him where we had met because my name did not ring a bell. I was furious but refreshed his memory and added the new information about his portion of the bill. He laughed and asked how many times I had used the "pay for my abortion" ruse to get money from men. There was nothing more to say.

I no longer grade on looks.

####### 17 ....

Must update my mandate for the next man I date.

Everybody does it. We all have a list, at least a mental one, that we carry around to determine if a person will be in our "yes" pile or the "oh, hell no!" box. I have such a list. Mine is more like a manifesto and it has served me well WHEN I follow it. Some of the declarations have been made out of sheer frustration but for the most part, experience has been an invaluable teacher in drafting a logical map to avoid pitfalls. Looking back, I am not surprised at all that it didn't work with Frank when I threw my own directions out.

Rule number 1: No more dating white guys.
Sounds controversial, but it is a very practical rule. While I am able to acknowledge that genetics can throw little curve balls here and there, the probability of my having a bunch of black babies with a white guy ... is currently zero.

This rule should have been pretty simple to follow. It wasn't like those times you see a little sign posted in a museum that says "don't touch" and you are compelled to do otherwise. But the cosmos lined up and brought Frank into my life. Didn't see it coming. Partially because at the time I was dating a beautiful black girl and mostly because I thought that Frank was gay.

Frank literally lived a stone's throw away from me, (if you can throw the length of a football field) in a very family-friendly subdivision. It was great to have a single, young, good-looking gay guy to hang around with. To go antique shopping with. To talk about gardening with and best of all, to gossip about the crazy neighbors. Like the ridiculously obsessive one who was running and panting away while she was nine months pregnant ... that had nothing, absolutely nothing, to do with her baby's well-being. We got along famously as we sat on the curb by the mailbox on the street (because sitting in chairs would have looked intentional) and trash-talked everybody in sight. Frank was, like every good gay guy, a very sympathetic ear and totally understood my reasons for wanting to end my relationship with my then girlfriend. He even went as far as suggesting what I should say to break it off. Such a nice guy.

It was the night of another one of our parties where we invited the other single neighbors and some friends over and Frank, as usual, was being a tremendous help in the kitchen. I was rinsing off dishes and he came up from behind and gave me a bear hug. Cute. He then kissed my neck. So sweet. Then his hands started off on a journey that they should never have willingly wanted to go. "You're gay, right?" would have gone over very badly, but thankfully at the time Frank was seven bottles of beer into the night. He clarified that he was not and after a few weird weeks, I said yes to giving a relationship with him a chance.

Rule number 2: No dating smokers.
Eeewwww ... sticky, slimy cigarette tongue. The only thing more repulsive than kissing a smoker in my mind, is kissing somebody with halitosis. There is nothing worse than being slobbered and then smelling that bad breath on your face as their saliva dries up. Easy rule to follow.

So why was I locking lips with a chain smoker? I could smell the smoke in his clothes, in his hair, on his skin and I couldn't get enough. Did all my years of inhaling secondhand smoke turn me into a nicotine fiend? I just assumed that I was growing so attracted to Frank that even the little red flags didn't matter. Besides, he had a nice big check mark next to Rule 3.

Rule number 3: No dating short guys.
Sorry. I don't make the rules. Apparently, I just decide which ones to follow. If it was "survival of the nicest mate" or "selection of the most reasonably adequate partner" then men under 5'5" would have no problem. Coming from a family that is relatively short demands that I have to look out for the next generation. It is not about me. It is all about the children. (Please feel free to direct any complains to Darwin's heirs so we can keep this moving.)

Frank was 6'4" and rugged. He reminded me of a rustic farmhand, or a lumberjack minus the flannel shirt. There was something very untamed and unapologetic about his height and size and the way he strode confidently through his world. I loved it and also loved that he also scored high marks for two other important strict charter requirements.

Rule number 4: No skinny guys.
This is relative. I am not a chubby chaser, but if the circumference of a man's thigh is significantly smaller than mine, I have no business being anywhere in the vicinity.

Rule number 5: No nasty nails.
No crazy "cocaine" little fingernail. All fingernails need to be the same length. No jacked-up toenails. Also, while it is not required for any man to have a pedicure, I don't think it is too much to ask for anyone to clean under their nails.

Rule number 6: No dating any man with a substance abuse problem.
Aaarrgghh ... how in the world ... ?! To be fair, it wasn't my fault for not recognizing that red flag. I just thought Frank was a very funny and an extremely friendly guy. Who knew he was a

functioning alcoholic who managed to maintain a consistent high for the nine months we dated? At first, I found it a little amusing that I constantly had to sober Frank up or drive us home. I thought it was very generous of me as his girlfriend to help him out of the car and into the house. Help him out of his clothes. Help him into bed. Remind him what he spent his money on the next morning. Drunken sex is funny the first time, and only the first time, around.

Rule number 7: No unsafe sex.
Well, we can just skip over that since I ignored it for over half a year.

Rule number 8: No dating any guy if their friends suck.
This is just good practice. In the early stages of dating, most people send out their ambassadors so you can only get a glimpse of the real deal if you spend time around their extended social circle. Chances are if you don't get along with them, you will not get along with him as time progresses.

Hmm. The pot smokers who didn't leave until all the food was gone should have clued me in. If not them, then the Neo-Nazi bitch, who refused to acknowledge that I occupied space in the physical realm, should have indicated that some of the people Frank spent time with were of a different mindset. If not her, then his roommate who would get so drunk that he would pass out and defecate all over the sofa. If not the sofa (which I refused to sit on ever again), I should have turned my attention to his lovely mother who said I was trying to get pregnant and have "an anchor baby" with her precious only son. Silly cow. Me, not her. All those red flags and still I was rolling in the sheets with Frank and sealing my fate to forever have these individuals traipse in and out of my future new world.

Rule number 9: No dating a man who cannot manage his money.
To be clear, I am not a gold digger. I am the very opposite. I get upset observing anybody's deliberate attempt to flaunt wealth. However, a man who cannot use money wisely is more infuriating. Pulling money out of your 401K to go to gamble because you have a "good feeling" about a set of lucky numbers is not a wise choice. Spending twenty dollars each and every single day on lotto scratch off tickets … not a responsible investment. Buying a double pack of anything (because you save a few cents) when you live alone and cannot consume half of the "great buy" before it spoils is very stupid.

We had fights about how he spent his money and bigger fights about waste. Frank was the kind of guy who would grab extra napkins because he paid for the burger. After his meal, he would throw a whole stack of clean napkins into the trash. One time we broke up over him leaving the faucet running as he brushed his teeth. I couldn't stand being the conservation police and have him mock me for taking navy showers or whine about me switching off lights in unoccupied rooms in the house.

Rule number 10: No dating emotionally manipulative men.
Excellent advice. However, I see no traces of that ever being applied.

I have to date a stable man to balance off some of my manic tendencies. I know this. I also know that I am easily manipulated by other people's emotions. Even the fake ones. I cannot watch certain commercials on TV because I will get misty eyed. I am aware that the people on the screen are actors but I tear up just the same. In the real world, people who cry at the drop of a hat, or fly into rages should not date. Ever. Frank knew good and well that his tears were like kryptonite and that I was powerless if we ever argued to the point where his eyes welled up or his voice wavered.

It took me four break-ups and make-ups to build up a tolerance to his tears when I discovered he was using sadness as a weapon. On our last and final day, I just walked away leaving him sobbing at his front door. I flinched a bit at the sniffling sounds behind me but stayed the course.

Months later I cringed at the recollection of ever having dated him and not abiding by my rules.

.... 18 ....

In my defense: The Grocery Method.

Don't go shopping if you are hungry. You will make decisions based on the growls in your stomach and wind up standing at the checkout line looking at your cart wondering how that pint of cherry amaretto ice cream was ever part of the plan. I can attest to many late nights of compulsive shopping choices that lead to a trash can full of spoiled fruit and vegetables. All those poor avocados didn't stand a chance. The same principle can be applied to dating if you have not engaged in sexual activity for an extended period of time. That is why I have sex with someone I know before I have sex with somebody new.

Objection! Misleading. The reader is drawing conclusions before all the evidence is presented.

Trevor sent a message after reading my profile and we instantly connected. We had so much in common, in that we both had unconventional taste in most things, especially in music. We exchanged less than a handful of emails sharing our favorite play lists and undiscovered artists before phone conversations started. I loved the sound of his voice. I had been on the dating site for a while and gone for a series of terrible coffees and dinners that I was beginning to lose hope until he came along with the promise of better dates to come.

Our first date was clumsy and giddy. We smiled too much and expressed our combined relief that we had both lived up to our individual profiles. He was even better looking in person. Very slim and athletic, but I wasn't going to hold that against him because everything else about him was sublime. It was going to be a problem.

We all know certain things about ourselves, even if we don't acknowledge those traits or behaviors willingly. For instance, I know I have a short temper that gets even shorter when dealing with indecisive people. Make a choice already. I know my curiosity puts me in harm's way when I find myself asking the question "what's the worst that could happen?" before attempting something stupid. I also know that, despite my best effort to curb the tendency, I am forever and always will be an optimist when it comes to new relationships. My excitement and enthusiasm can be overwhelming to anyone I set my sights on and unfortunately, in many instances, the individual I am interested in is turned off. Knowing this, I attempted to avert that inevitability with Trevor when I felt my eagerness creeping in.

I hear that there are people who keep a little black book of former lovers whom they can call up during a dry spell. I would love to be a fly on the wall during that first phone call to set up the tryst. I don't have a list of former conquests. What I do have is a man whom I can call at anytime to tide me over when I am between relationships. Being a married man, his discretion was something I could rely on.

Objection. Badgering.

Yes, the same old man I mentioned before. How many married men am I supposed to be sleeping with? I have known him for over 15 years and in that time my body betrayed all its secrets. Can I just say, the only thing better than a secret is knowing? Having sex with The Old Man was a sure thing. I knew before, during and after that I would be totally satisfied and that takes a lot of pressure off attaining an orgasm.

The Old Man was aware that I was online and actively dating, I just had not shared that I was relying on his body as insurance against my choices. I liked sitting across from a new date and focusing on the conversation at hand without having to quell a riot in my panties. Thanks to him, I could just say goodnight and drive safely home. The Old Man was actually performing a very useful function in my life because without him, I would have probably racked up an absurd number of partners.

Objection! Hearsay. The number of partners has never been disclosed; as such terms like "slut" should be stricken from the record.

And so the day came when Trevor invited me to spend the night. I had stalled for what I felt was a respectable number of dates (because I had heard all my life that good girls don't give it up that fast). The Old Man was happy to oblige my midweek midday request. Six hours later, I was confirming directions to Trevor's house.

Permission to treat the reader as hostile.

I will concede that having sex with two men on the same day sounds a little distasteful. There were extenuating circumstances. First of all, I already explained "the grocery method." I don't use this method frequently; it is only applied when I am really interested in somebody. Sounds counterintuitive to have sex with someone other than the person you really like, but ...

Secondly, Trevor changed our schedule. Our sleepover was supposed to occur over the weekend. HE brought it forward three days. If he had stuck to the schedule, I would have had plenty of time to get myself in order with The Old Man. Third, I was excited that he spontaneously changed plans, and didn't want to take "no" for an answer, so I didn't stop to think what my actions from earlier in the afternoon would look like on paper the next day.

The following weeks were a little tricky as I waited for my period. I had used protection but that doesn't register when looking at a calendar date that should have a nice "X" running through it. The idea that I was potentially about to live out a Maury Povich scenario was unbearable. How does a DNA testing conversation start?

Verdict? How can you be ready to render judgment when I haven't even begun closing arguments?

.... 19 ....

The A-1 Steak Sauce Incident.

I've had all types of break-ups. The deafening silence that turns into indifference and then disdain. The furious self-defense, which can only be conveyed when screaming at a pitch that dogs alone can hear. The polite exit where each party discreetly increases the distance between themselves and a slowly fading romance, until any evidence that love occurred is all but vanished. The vindictive text message breakup that leaves you wondering if they are stupid and cannot spell or just plain lazy. Never in my wildest dreams did I ever imagine that I would be in a breakup that would wind up with me behind bars or dead … okay, that is a little dramatic … would wind up in jail or, in the hospital.

How Huey and I met is not spectacular; what is fascinating is how we ended things. We both wanted to be very civilized about it when it was determined that we weren't compatible after all, and had come to the conclusion that we would remain friends. To show there were no hard feelings, Huey even offered to cook our last supper to symbolically bring our relationship period to an end and usher in the friendship era.

My roommate told me to decline. It was too soon to walk into a room with the remains of a slain relationship festering in the corner and pretend not to notice the stench. I thought otherwise. I believed we would have a lovely dinner, mock each other a little bit over the silly fight that finally tore us irreparably apart and then toast to each other's good health and go our separate ways until our paths crossed in the future. Besides, the dinner menu sounded delicious. Huey was a great cook; the ten extra pounds of weight I was lugging around could attest to that.

I was only about 15 minutes late so I couldn't understand the hostility that Huey answered the door with. It had been established that when I said "be there in a minute" it meant I was on the way and might be late. It was a figure of speech. There was no way I could possibly get to his house in a minute when I lived a good 20 minutes away, so why was he pointing out the time and explaining that he had been slaving over the grill and dinner was now ruined. I was taking off my heavy coat and scarf and noticed that he had started eating without me and was a good portion into his meal. The steak on his plate looked juicy and smelled divine. The potatoes au gratin looked creamy and delicious as always and the asparagus gleamed from the tiny bit of olive oil he would brush them with after steaming.

What is he talking about ruined?
I am not going to miss his melodrama at all.

Apparently, it was a self-service night because Huey returned to his plate and continued his meal in silence. I tried to be bright and cheery as I complimented all the wonderful aromas that filled the house as I made my way to the kitchen to help myself. I was starving. I had skipped lunch in anticipation of this meal.

Where IS my meal?

The kitchen sink was full of soaking dishes. I could clearly see the pots and pans where the potatoes and asparagus had been prepared, and outside on the patio the grill was still smoking. I called out to Huey asking where my steak was and he grunted back that he had left it on the grill to stay warm.

What the hell?!

I opened the lid of the grill to find a scorched piece of meat helplessly giving off its last bits of fat to the fire. He hadn't even tried to turn the flame down. I took what was left of a previously beautiful cut of meat into the kitchen and preceded to scrape away the burnt portions. It was a sad attempt at a rescue. All I could do was cut into the hunk of dried up meat and hope to salvage the edible center section. It was too far-gone and badly overcooked. I was able to reclaim only about six bites of beef.

The entire time the rescue operation was in progress, Huey was silently watching TV. I could hear his cutlery and imagined his steak knife slicing effortlessly into his buttery steak. I was not going to make a scene.

I am not going to make a scene.

I looked down at my plate with a few chunks of dry tasteless flesh and decided to make the best of it. Some black pepper and A-1 Steak sauce might help. Huey walked into the kitchen and didn't say a word about the situation on my plate. His only comment was that he wanted to grab the steak sauce when I was through with it as he rifled through the fridge to pull out a cold beer. I finished dousing my sad meal, replaced the cap onto the bottle and walked into the living room hoping to quietly steal a taste of potato off his plate.

Moments later a barrage of insults were being hurled at me from the kitchen.

What the hell now?

I walked into the kitchen and I couldn't contain the loud gasp that came out of my mouth. The entire kitchen was covered, floor to ceiling, in reddish brown sauce. Huey was standing at the kitchen counter furiously screaming that only a moron doesn't screw a bottle cap back onto a bottle. I looked at him in puzzlement as I observed the spray of sauce all over the white counters and the appliances and the floor and the window and the sliding glass door that stood between this mess and the still smoking grill outside.

HE is calling ME the moron?
What kind of a moron shakes a bottle with his entire body?
Was he jumping up and down?
Why didn't he stop shaking the bottle after the first spill?
Did he think the bottle cap would magically spring off the counter where it was resting and refasten itself if he continued to agitate the bottle?
Is he joking?

I smiled at Huey, as he demanded a response. I quietly told him that I did not refasten the bottle cap because he was about to use the sauce. It was obvious that it wasn't fastened and merely sitting on top of the bottle. I also offered that he had walked in to find me shaking the bottle so I thought it strange that he felt it needed a double shake. I also said that I thought it was curious that he was shaking the condiment in the kitchen when his plate was in the living room. Huey was not amused and snapped angrily that I needed to grab a dishrag to clean my mess.

MY mess?!

It was funny to have a giant of a man covered in sauce screaming obscenities at me. He got more enraged as my smile broadened and my silence jeered back at his noise. Then I saw the look in his eyes. I recognized why we call it instinct when danger makes an appearance. I did not hesitate.

I grabbed my keys and headed for the door, as Huey was a few paces behind shouting that I was not going anywhere until I fixed things. I made it into my car and hit the lock, automatically locking the remaining three doors. Huey was at the driver's side window with his face turning red and saying nothing. He was trying to open the door with one hand as he slammed his other fist against the glass. He couldn't understand why the door wasn't opening. I could have told him it was probably a design flaw (or consideration) that the lock on driver's side did not retract completely into the door paneling as it did on the other doors; so it always gave the impression that the driver's side door was unlocked. That tall lock was tormenting him something fierce. He walked back into the house. I was not going to wait to find out what he was retrieving. I started my trusty car with its perfectly designed locks and began my retreat. Huey raced back out and lunged himself at the side of my car grabbing hold of the luggage rack on the roof of the station wagon.

Who designed this clown car anyhow?
I have never once used that stupid luggage rack and now I have a crazy man dangling from it!
He is going to have to let go because I am NOT stopping.

Huey's driveway was narrow and long. I reversed very slowly while glancing simultaneously at the rear view mirror and at Huey. He was basically escorting (or trying to carry) my car down the driveway. I made it to the mailbox and was about to shift into drive when Huey released the roof rack and hurried to the front of my car. I shifted into drive and very lightly bumped him. He did not move.

I reversed my station wagon the length of his property and sat there for a moment observing the giant blocking the road ahead of me. There were cars parked on the right side of the street reducing my options to two choices; climb the curb to my left and drive around him, or, step on the accelerator and drive over him.

The songs on the radio were playing along happily in a strange and surreal disconnect to the drama that was still unfolding. I was shaking uncontrollably. I couldn't tell if I was freezing from the cold outside or full of adrenaline. Huey was still standing akimbo in the middle of the street, red as ever. He was yelling again so I turned the radio up and hummed along to calm my nerves while I decided what I was going to do. I revved my engine.

He is going to have to move because I am not stopping.
Why is he not moving?
I am NOT stopping!
... this guy is not moving!
Is he insane?

My car would have made contact with Huey if he had not taken a few quick steps to the left. I looked in the rearview. He was still standing there except his hands were now on his head. I guess neither of us had realized until this moment, that between the two of us, I was the crazy one.

.... 20 ....

Never ever have I ever.

Old men have worms. Once you let them in, you can't get rid of them that easy. Even if they are physically gone, a part of them detaches and quietly boroughs its way into your core to find a home. I had no idea what I was setting myself up for 15 years ago.

It was actually sixteen August 2011 ... dang it!

I never thought I'd be "that girl" who messed around with a married man. If that wasn't bad enough, I became that-girl-who-is-messing-around-with-a-married-man-pretending-not-to-see-the-shock-and-disappointment-on-anybody's-face when I disclosed exactly how long I have been in a situation with him.

Refusing to call it a relationship somehow, at least in my mind, gives me an out because it suggests that I am not a willing participant in this affair and that my involvement is a byproduct of a grander, more elaborate and intricate scheme. I have rattled off on numerous occasions why the benefits outweigh the uncomfortable stares, giving reasons ranging from "he fixes my car," to "he helped renovate my condo," to "he takes care of my cats when I am traveling."

That last one justified an extra year when one of my cats was terribly sick. He helped me give her medication twice a day, he was with me at the animal emergency room, and when it was time to put her down seven months later, it was he who helped pick me off the floor to save me from the puddle of tears I was flailing about in.

It is NOT a stupid excuse ... people stay together "for the kids" all the time.

Okay, maybe all my reasons are actually excuses. They just sound so much better than uttering the words *I love him*. I would also lose the tiny ounce of credibility I have left that is desperately hanging on and would rather be thought of as a cold, callous bitch than a silly, lovesick puppy.

Anger walks away. Love stays. Maybe stupid also stays. All I know is that I need to find that piece of him that is lodged in my soul and rip it out because if this is not love, I am afraid to find out what the real thing looks like.

The closest I got to an exit was a couple of months ago. I was having dinner with a close friend and The Dirty Old Man came up in conversation. I was explaining how I didn't get much sleep the previous night because his snoring was keeping me up and I was bleary-eyed at a meeting that afternoon. She asked how often he spent the night and I was busily replying that at times he was at my place for the entire week. What came next was a very simple statement that set into motion a chain of events and actions that I could never have envisioned. She said, "That man is not married" as she took a sip of her drink.

My entire brain shut down and my only response was to empty my own glass into my mouth in a fruitless attempt to uncover a defensive retort beneath the rum flavored ice cubes. Taking my silence as a cue, she went on to say that no married woman would put up with her husband going to have a sleepover with his chick on the side for over a decade. She then suggested that he was pretending to be married so that he could avoid a genuine commitment with me and used the old "I don't want to hurt my wife" trick to keep me at a manageable distance. I sat back in my chair and digested all this new, but very obvious (to anybody but me) information.

Why does the truth taste so bad?

That night as he snored contentedly next to me, I could think of little else. Fifteen years ... SIXteen years, and I know nothing about the man in my bed. If his wife were to show up at my front door (if he in fact had a wife), I wouldn't even be aware who the axe-wielding-wild-eyed-screaming-assailant was. He knew everything about me, my family, my friends, my job, my vacation itinerary so he can pick me up from the airport and take care of the cats ... he is so sweet that way ...

FOCUS!

What did I know about him? How old is he? Where does he live? I had to find out. Never, ever, did I think I was the type of woman who would sneak into a man's wallet. Here I was though, hunched over in the dark with a pile of clothes trying to quietly figure out which pocket of his cargo pants held the prize. I finally found the wallet and snuck off to the kitchen.

My hands were trembling. I was caught in the middle of fear and escalating rage as I looked at his address. I knew the road. I now also knew why we had to drive extra miles in the opposite direction to the other Home Depot instead of the one I frequented. He lives less than four minutes away. I tiptoed back to the bedroom to retrieve my cell phone to take a photo of his driver's license because I did not want to risk writing his information on paper.

Dang it! WHO at BlackBerry decided that the camera function needed sound effects?

The sound made by my camera app was unmistakable and was

as clear as a bell ringing into a quiet night. I stood there looking at the blurry image that was captured not able to make out any text and wondered if it was worth another snap. Two more fuzzy images later and I was navigating my way back to the bedroom as I contemplated whether I had made a mistake not getting an iPhone. My thoughts were interrupted by the sound of silence. What happened to the snoring? I had my phone (with the keypad still illuminated and casting a blue glow onto me) in one hand, and a wallet in the other. What would I say if he was sitting up when I walked into the room?

Never, ever, had I ever thought I would use my body to conceal and transport contraband. With one swift move, I tucked his wallet under my right breast and walked into the room. It was dark and my eyes had not adjusted from the florescent kitchen light. I couldn't tell if he was asleep but I couldn't risk assuming he was. There was no way around trying to get the wallet back into his trousers if he was awake. With his wallet still stashed between my breast and pounding chest, I returned to the kitchen for a glass of water. I had determined that my best course of action was to try NOT to be quiet because then he would hopefully not be suspicious. Cell phone in one hand, glass of tap water in the other, wallet hitching a ride under breast, I tried to casually walk back into the room. He was awake.

Did I wake him in my attempt not to be sneaky? Wouldn't that be funny?

I pretended to stumble into the wicker clothes' basket (that was nowhere near me) so I could pull all his clothes to the floor and use that opportunity to stick his wallet back into his pocket.

SOOO many pockets! There should be a rule about the number of pockets on an article of clothing.

As an insurance policy I muttered out loud and when he asked what was going on, I tried to sound disinterested and casually said his wallet fell out of his pants when I was putting his clothes back on the hamper. When he repeated my statement as a question, I casually asked which pocket he wanted me to put it in. He didn't respond so I declared that he would find it in one of his back pockets. To complete the casual-unsuspicious-act, I sat on the edge of the bed next to him and offered him some water while I tried to sound nonchalant about taking advantage of the time difference to instant message family in Kenya. He didn't want any water so I took a sip and pretended to send an instant message but that didn't work for long because I needed the sound alert of an incoming message.

Thanks Research In Motion! If he kills me I am going to destroy your precious phone.

I slid back under the covers. My eyes had now adjusted to the darkness and I lay in bed realizing that light was streaming in through the widows into the hallway. I had been framed in light the entire time. He could see me (if his eyes were open) extract his wallet from its fleshy carriage and drop it on the pile of clothes and then decide to tip the basket over. My heart pounded loudly and I was parched and regretted leaving the glass on his side of the bed.

HIS SIDE? This is not his bed!
Push him out of it and ask him why he never mentioned he could walk to his house from here without breaking a sweat!
All those times he said he just left his house and was driving my way and would be there in half an hour.
What was he doing with twenty-seven of those minutes?

I needed more than an address to confront him with, because I had used a license that displayed an old street address for close to two years. I lay there outlining a plan of action and trying not to focus on the fact that he wasn't snoring. He was probably awake and probably wondering what was going on.

Never, ever did I think that I would be canceling a business meeting to research the man I was having sex with. The Cobb County tax assessor's office website revealed that the address on his driver's license did in fact match the property a few neighborhoods from my own.

So, THAT'S his wife's name, huh?
So that's where she works?
Could that be her photo?

At least I confirmed the address was accurate and he lived there with his wife. But maybe they only had joint title and now one of them lived there alone, or the property was a rental that they both claimed a stake in. He could be divorced and still pretending to be married. I called Cobb County records and was directed to the Courts. Magistrate Court could not locate his name and suggested he had been married in a different county. Fulton County Courts could not find any record of either party. They in turn pointed me to Vital Records in DeKalb County, which kept track of all marriages, births and deaths for the entire state and indicated they could research if he was married outside the State of Georgia.

The form required information I did not have. Year of marriage. Her full maiden name. Year of divorce. It also contained information I did not want to share. My full name. My address and signature. Relationship to parties I was researching. I would have to attack this problem from a different angle.

Never ever did I ever think that I was the type of person who was willing to hire a private investigator.

·······

Don't Cry Because It's Over, Smile Because It Happened
– Dr. Seuss

·······

Every good story has to come to an end to make room for another. Thank you for investing your time. If you'd like to share your thoughts, please feel free to post a note on the blog at www.relationsh-t.com

I hope you enjoyed this first book and are looking forward to the second: "All banged up, but still standing. A true love story." making its debut in 2012 (that is the plan for now).

All the best until next time,

Christina Nkirote Mugambi.